After the challenges of life in the Far East, Desmond Malone came to London with his family. He attended a Jesuit college and then worked in the Bank of England for forty years. On retirement Desmond became a City of London guide. He now guides regularly in St Paul's Cathedral.

To Anna
with best wishes
Danny
November '06

TURBULENT TIMES IN THE FAR EAST

The Story of the Malone Family, 1893–1946

TURBULENT TIMES IN THE FAR EAST

The Story of the Malone Family, 1893–1946

Desmond Malone

ATHENA PRESS
LONDON

TURBULENT TIMES IN THE FAR EAST:
The Story of the Malone Family, 1893–1946
Copyright © Desmond Malone 2006

ISBN 1 84401 702 8

First Published 2006 by
ATHENA PRESS
Queen's House, 2 Holly Road
Twickenham TW1 4EG
United Kingdom

Printed for Athena Press

To my dear wife Margaret and our children,
Michael, Patricia, Anthony and Helen.

Author's Note

I was initially prompted to write this account of my early life primarily to satisfy the curiosity of my children to know something of my activities as a boy in the Far East, before and during the Second World War. A second reason for undertaking this exercise was the belief that if a person has a story of his life to tell, he should do so, as it enables those who come after him to be able to share in the experiences, which he has encountered.

In preparing my story, so many years afterwards, I have been able to stand back from my early life and see it more objectively and with a mature eye, thus getting a more clear understanding of the events that my family and I lived through in those troubled times. Furthermore, having embarked on this enterprise, I have taken the opportunity to widen its scope to cover the life and times of the Malone family as a whole during their years in the Far East.

I hope those who read this account will enjoy the book and that some will have their eyes opened to the turbulent events in the Far East during the first part of the twentieth century, since these happenings have not always received the prominence in this country that they undoubtedly deserve.

Acknowledgements

I am very grateful to Major Chapman, the curator of the Green Howards Museum, Richmond, North Yorkshire, for the help he has given me and for the interest he has shown in providing me with details of my grandfather Richard Malone's years in the army serving with the Green Howards in the latter part of the nineteenth century. I wish to thank him very much for all he has done.

Thanks are due also to Father Hans Boerraker of the St Joseph's Missionary Society, Mill Hill, who kindly consulted his archives to provide me with details of the lives of four Mill Hill priests whom we had known when they were with us in Santo Tomas internment camp in Manila.

I am greatly indebted to the Columban Fathers of Solihull, West Midlands and in particular, Father Denis Carter, for sending me the publication *Columban Martyrs of Malate*, which describes the heroic work of the Columban priests in Manila in the Malate parish, headed by Father Patrick Kelly during those terrible years under Japanese occupation. A copy of the publication was unobtainable in this country and Father Carter needed to order one from the Philippines. I wish to thank him sincerely for the trouble he has taken on my behalf.

I should mention also that my sister, Moira, who died in 1985, wrote a brief account of our early life which has been most helpful to me in this narrative.

Having made up my mind to write this story, I am pleased to say I gained the support of my wonderful family. My daughter, Patricia, engaged herself with some interest in typing the subsequent drafts. My younger daughter, Helen, cast a discerning eye over my narrative, giving me constructive suggestions, most of which I have adopted.

My two sons, Michael and Anthony, have voiced their general comments, which I have duly noted. I should like, therefore, to thank my family for the interest they have shown and the help they have given me in their different ways.

However, I wish to give a special thank you to my dear wife, Margaret, who has borne the brunt of my preoccupation from start to finish. She gave me the support and encouragement I needed to make a start. She kindly typed my first draft. Without her love and support, this account may never have been written.

Contents

Author's Note   ix

Acknowledgements   x

Setting the Scene; the Early Days:
   The Army 1865–1886   15

The Move to China   21

The Next Generation   32

The Build-up to China's War with Japan   45

The Sino–Japanese War   50

Moira Visits England   61

A Trip to Haiphong   65

Life in Canton   70

Japan Enters the Second World War   79

Internment – 1942   87

Internment – 1943   116

Internment – 1944   132

Freedom at Last   152

A New Life   179

Internees in China   184

Sixty Years On   193

Bibliography   202

Setting the Scene; the Early Days
The Army 1865–1886

The story I shall be telling is that of the Malone family in the Far East. In order to set the scene for that story I shall take you back to the birth of my paternal grandfather, Richard John Joseph Malone, who first saw the light of day in the St Andrew's parish of Dublin in the year 1846. After a sound education, in 1865 at the age of nineteen years, Richard joined the 1st Battalion of the Yorkshire Regiment, 19th Foot, the Green Howards.

The 19th Foot had been serving in India since 1857. After his basic training in 1865, Richard joined his regiment in the North West Frontier at Peshawar, a town in a mountainous area of the Punjab, known as the Black Mountain, on the edge of the Afghan border. This mountainous region was inhabited by fiercely independent Islamic tribesmen who frequently made incursions into the valleys below, targeting those villages under British protection and destroying them. One such occasion took place in July 1868, which prompted the Black Mountain campaign. Early one morning, a large force of 10,000 men were assembled at Oghi to beat this menace. The Green Howards played a leading role in the exercise. So successful was the operation that by nightfall all resistance from the tribesmen had ceased. The outcome of this skirmish was that it brought a few years respite before any further trouble arose from that quarter. The Green Howards returned to Rawalpindi where they had been stationed prior to their posting to Peshawar in 1865.

Those soldiers who had taken part received the Indian Service Medal with clasp 'North West Frontier'. Private Richard Malone was fortunate, so early on in his military career, to be among those who saw action and must have been proud to have received his medal.

After spending a good fourteen years in India, the 19th Foot returned to England, docking at Portsmouth in December 1871. While stationed at Aldershot in 1877, Richard married a widow, Mary Agnes O'Mally (née Cosgrove) at Farnborough parish church in October of that year.

The Green Howards were due for a tour of the colonies. In November 1877 the regiment left Portsmouth for Bermuda. During their stay there in 1880, the first of four surviving Malone children of the marriage, Agnes Mary Walburger, was born. In November of that year the regiment moved to Halifax, Nova Scotia, from a comfortable temperature of 78°F in the shade to the breath-freezing 15°F. In December 1882, my future father, Richard Henry, was born. From Canada, the 19th moved to Malta in March 1884. In the summer of that year preparations were being made for a possible expedition to be led by General Wolseley to relieve General Charles Gordon, besieged in Khartoum by the Mahdi, the fanatical ruler of the Sudan. Orders were given to the 19th to reinforce the garrison in Egypt. They arrived in Alexandria from Malta in August.

The reason that Gordon was in this predicament was that he had been despatched to the Sudan in January 1884 by Gladstone's Cabinet in London with specific instructions to arrange for the evacuation of British and Egyptian Army personnel. Gordon disobeyed these orders as he judged it would be wrong to withdraw and abandon the country to the mercy of the Mahdi's dervishes. The position was that the Mahdi, resentful of Britain's involvement in his country, had led an uprising supported by his slave trader followers. The regime had reintroduced oppressive measures on its people and brought back the slave trade, which Gordon himself had abolished whilst Governor of the Sudan a few years previously. Having resolved to stay, Gordon called for reinforcements to overthrow the fanatical leader. Gladstone and his Liberal Government were taken aback at Gordon's stance and resisted any pressure to go to his aid. By May, Gordon was cut-off in Khartoum. Eventually, the Government relented and by September Wolseley was given the go-ahead to mount the rescue operation. He set out from the borders of Egypt for the 800 miles advance to Khartoum. However, when the first British troops reached Khartoum on the 28 January 1885, it was too late; the city had fallen two days before and General Gordon was dead. At home he became a national martyr and many held Gladstone responsible for his death. General Wolseley was instructed to abandon the Sudan and bring the troops back to Egypt.

The Green Howards, who thought they had been called to Egypt to assist in the Gordon relief expedition, were to remain in Alexandria until March 1885 and missed all the excitement. They did, however, see some action. They were ordered to go upstream to Aswan to form part of the Egyptian Field Frontier Force which established its HQ in that town. The Force was composed of British regiments supported by Egyptian units. In May, it was learnt that the Mahdi had made plans to invade Egypt. It was necessary then to return to the Sudan to forestall any invasion. The Frontier Force crossed the border at Wadi Halfa and marched a hundred miles south along the banks of the Nile. They deployed themselves within a short distance of the Sudanese village of Ginnis, where the dervishes had concentrated their forces. As the mixed British and Egyptian force advanced on Ginnis, and following an exchange of fire between the combatants, the dervishes could be seen fleeing their stronghold while the British guns continued to direct their fire on the escaping enemy. An important victory was won, as it ended the immediate threat of the Sudanese invasion of Egypt. This engagement at Ginnis in December 1885 was an historic occasion in that it was the last time in action that the British Army wore their famous scarlet tunics. Sergeant Richard Malone had taken part in the assault and was awarded the Egyptian Medal and the Khedive's Bronze Star, as were all his comrades who had served in the conflict. The Green Howards returned to Egypt and by May 1886 were back in Aswan.

It was while stationed in Aswan that Richard and his family left for England, as his service in the army was coming to an end. In August 1886 he received his discharge papers at Gosport at the age of forty, with the rank of sergeant. He and his family settled in Loughborough, Leicestershire, where Richard obtained a job as a club steward. In 1887 Maud Margaret was born followed by George Thomas Sylvester in 1892.

The following year an opportunity arose for the Malone family to go to China. Richard's decision to start a new life on the other side of the world introduced a radically different dimension to the lives of his wife and young family as they settled in their new home beyond the seas.

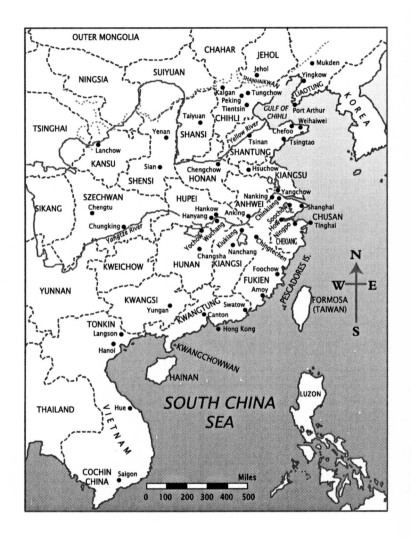

from Christopher Hibbert,
The Dragon Wakes: China and the West 1793–1911.

The Move to China

In 1893 Richard John answered an advertisement for a post in the Customs Service in Hankow, China, and was successful in his application. At that time the Chinese Maritime Customs was an international service managed mainly by British officials. To take up his post, Richard, together with his family, set sail for China in that year. Their new home was a town situated on the north bank of the Yangtze River, some 600 miles inland from the coast in the Hupeh Province.

For over one hundred years before the Malones reached China's shores, the relationship between the Chinese and the foreigners living in their country had deteriorated to an all-time low. For centuries China, under her emperors, had regarded herself as self-sufficient and had no desire to trade with other nations. Her only concession to foreign interest in China was to allow the Portuguese, in the middle of the sixteenth century, to establish themselves on the offshore island of Macao, as a link between East and West. Tensions had arisen in the eighteenth century by the pressing demands of Western nations, headed by Britain, for Chinese trade. China had reluctantly allowed a small enclave of foreign traders, mainly British, to deal with a few specially-licensed Chinese merchants in Canton, an important South China city, but they were confined to a small area of the shoreline of that city. These foreigners could only operate in the autumn and early winter each year. Many other irksome restrictions were imposed on them. In spite of these constraints and the modest amount of legal trade transacted, these traders, in the nineteenth century, began to amass great wealth. The source of this wealth was the illicit trade in opium. Chinese officials turned a blind eye to this trade as they were lining their pockets, through immense bribes, to enable the illegal transactions to take place in defiance of the Emperor's commands. China was determined to stamp out this trade in opium and took ruthless measures to try and eradicate it. Britain's answer was to declare war on China over this issue in 1839.

The Chinese were unequal to the struggle and hostilities ceased in 1842. By the Treaty of Nanking, Hong Kong was surrendered to Britain in perpetuity and Britain was granted ports on the Chinese mainland in which trade could be carried on between the two nations unhindered. Other foreign countries gained similar rights.

Further clashes with China followed the first opium war, with more rights and privileges conceded by China to the foreign powers. In some of the treaty ports, 'concessions' or areas of land were marked out and rented by foreign governments who sublet to their nationals. In others there were 'settlements', where foreign residents rented land and property directly from Chinese landlords. Whichever form the treaty ports took they deprived the Chinese government of authority over large areas in many cities and towns within China. Foreigners ruled their own settlements, administered their own laws, controlled their own police and ran the Customs Service. A deep-seated resentment was felt by the Chinese people at the humiliation they had received at the hands of the 'foreign devils'.

The Chinese are a resilient and practical race. On a personal level, they would work well for any foreigner if treated fairly and honestly. As a servant and often with his extended family, if looked after well, he would be faithful to his foreign employer. The Malone family, who were to live for generations in China, found this to be true.

Shortly after their arrival in Hankow, Richard Henry, aged ten years, was sent to boarding school in Shanghai at the Jesuit college, St Francis Xavier (SFX). Agnes and Maud (known as Aggie and Maudie) attended a convent in Hankow. George initially went to the convent with his sisters and later went to Shanghai to SFX, the school which Richard had attended. .

Richard had enjoyed his years at school in Shanghai. When he left in 1900 he had received a good education under the Jesuits and was a competent French speaker. His father obtained a position for Richard on the Peking Hankow Railway through the good offices of a French friend working on that railway. The foreigners, i.e. the British, French and Germans, were each responsible for a section of the railway they were building for the Chinese. Richard joined the French section.

Maudie left school in Hankow and, after a secretarial course, joined the Asiatic Petroleum Company (APC), a subsidiary of Shell Mex. She was very artistic and a talented painter.

Aggie, when a small girl, had been knocked down by a carriage in Loughborough, where the family were living before they left for China. One of her legs was badly damaged, which resulted in the injured leg being shorter than the other. Her mobility throughout her life was very restricted. When she left school, for some months she did clerical work in a post office but later remained at home, teaching adult students English and French.

George worked as an accountant after leaving school. He was a keen footballer and played every Saturday afternoon. A sturdy six-footer, he weighed at one time as much as twenty stone. For many years he played a skilful powerful game for his team as fullback.

Towards the close of the nineteenth century, China had more to contend with than the hated Western foreigner. Another spectre on the Chinese horizon was Japan's desire for territorial expansion. She, at first, cast envious eyes on Korea, a country subject to the overlordship of the Emperor of China. After considerable friction with China, in 1894 the Sino–Japanese war broke out over Korea. Japan's military superiority was overwhelming and a peace treaty was signed within a year. China was forced to give up her claims to Korea and Japan gained Formosa (Taiwan). The Boxer Rebellion of 1900 gave Japan another opportunity to expand territorially. This uprising was instigated by the Empress Dowager of China. An anti-foreign force besieged the foreign legations in Peking and murdered European missionaries and large numbers of Chinese converts to Christianity. An international force managed to restore order but Imperial Russia, ostensibly helping to deal with the rising, occupied the province of Manchuria. When the situation returned to normal, Russia showed little sign of evacuating the area. She seemed to have her sights on Korea also. Japan scotched any such ambitions by attacking Russia in 1904, decisively defeating her on all fronts. Russia evacuated Manchuria and recognised Japan's exclusive right to administer Korea. Most important of all, the South Manchurian railway passed into the Japanese sphere of influence. All these encroachments by Japan were to have a devastating effect on China in years to come.

In the early 1900s the Manchu dynasty was growing weak and crumbling. Nationalism and republicanism were starting to engage the minds of the Chinese people. Dr Sun Yat-sen, a young medical doctor, had for many years preached national revolution. His immediate aim was to bring the downfall of the dynasty, his long-term objective was to free China, once and for all, from foreign domination and lead a united country on the road to democracy. In 1911 Dr

Sun and his followers overthrew the Manchu regime and set in train the establishment of a republican form of government with Canton, in South China, as their capital. However, before the new government had consolidated its position, one disaffected leading military figure of the erstwhile Manchu dynasty named Yuan Shihkai, who was in control of the armed forces in the North, declared himself Emperor Hung Hsien on 1 January 1916, in the hope of being the first in a long line of a new dynasty. His aspirations came to nothing. In less than three months he was unseated and the government in Peking fell into the hands of warlords, who set up regional regimes in various provinces throughout China and fought among themselves for personal gain. They plunged the country into chaos. Dr Sun and his followers withdrew to Canton, but, at long last, in 1917 formally founded their revolutionary government.

An important part of Dr Sun's strategy to unite China was his need to defeat the warlords. From his capital in Canton, a northern expedition was to be launched to this end. As we shall see below, new unwanted developments in the country muddied the waters and delayed the start of the expedition.

The new disturbing element for China was the arrival in 1920 of the Russian Bolsheviks following the Russian Revolution of 1917. They soon formed the Chinese Communist Party which had its first congress in Shanghai in 1921. At the suggestion of the Russians an agreement was reached between them and Dr Sun in 1923 that, for the sake of national unity, the Chinese Communist Party should join the Nationalist Party (the Kuomintang) and accept Dr Sun's leadership. This agreement Dr Sun accepted in good faith. However, he died in 1925 and his national government now came under the direction of Chiang Kai-shek. Chiang had no illusions about the Communists. As early as March 1924 in a letter to one of his colleagues, copies of which were circulated among members of the Kuomintang Central Standing Committee, he stated, quite plainly, his view that the Russian Communist Party could not be trusted. He went on to say that in its dealings with China, the Russians had only one aim, namely to turn the Chinese Communist Party into an instrument for Soviet Russia's own use. Chiang's uncompromising view of Communist aims would be vindicated with the passage of time.

The preparation for the northern expedition was now in the hands of Chiang as the successor to Dr Sun. After stabilising the southern provinces of Kwantung and Kwangsi, following anti-communist disturbances in the army in July 1926, Chiang felt able to launch his campaign against the warlords and advanced north from Canton. The Nationalists made such rapid progress in that year, taking Wuchang in October and Nanchang in November, towns either side of the Yangtze River, that the warlords began to lose heart. From then onwards they did not present a serious problem for Chiang. However, a more dangerous and pressing situation was the activity of the

Communists within the ranks of the Nationalists. In 1927, after Chiang's forces had occupied Hankow, Chinese crowds – egged on and supported by the Communists – demonstrated against the foreign nationals in the city and the concessions they administered there. Such was the disturbance that British women and children were taken by naval gunboats upstream on the Yangtze River to safety. They remained under the protection of the Royal Navy until it was safe to return to Hankow.

Apart from this precautionary evacuation of women and children, the political and military turmoil which was affecting China at this time had not greatly touched the lives of the Malone family, nor indeed any other foreigners in China. It was not until Japan entered the scene in mainland China that the lives of many foreign nationals, but more particularly the Chinese people themselves, were affected by events in that country. But this was still a few years off.

It was the policy of the APC to send their employees on home leave every five years for an extended holiday. Maudie, together with her brothers and sister, set off for England early in 1921. They knew a priest among the Passionist Fathers of St Joseph's church, Highgate, North London, and they sought his advice on any Irish Catholic families in the parish with whom they might meet. They were directed to no. 18 Cholmley Park, Highgate, the home of the O'Donnells.

William Joseph O'Donnell, the father of the family,

an Irishman from Limerick City, at that time about fifty-one years of age, had come over from Ireland in 1888 at the age of eighteen years to take two examinations. One was for the Civil Service and the other for the London County Council (LCC), which was to come into being on 1 January 1889. He was an intelligent lad and quite adept at taking exams. In his schooldays he had sat a public examination in Italian and come first in the whole of Ireland (a medal denoting the achievement is still held by the family). He came second in the Civil Service exam and fourth in the LCC exam. He decided to join the LCC and in 1925 became the chief officer of the Public Control Department. He only had a few months to enjoy his promotion. He died the same year at the age of fifty-five.

In 1895 William had married Emily Constance Anne Downie, an English girl, at St Joseph's church, Highgate – they were both twenty-five-years-old. They had five children, all born in Highgate. Gladys Ellaline Mary Cecilia was born in 1896 (Moira and Desmond's future mother). Maud Madeline Mary Gabriel was born in 1899, she remained single. Desmond Eugene was born in 1905. In due time he was to marry Chrissie Masterman. Beryl Mary came into the world in 1908. She married Cecil George Fitt in 1929; there were two children of the marriage, Deirdre and Jennifer. Cecile Claire was born in 1910. She married Dermot Kilgallin in 1936. They had two children, Kevin and Claire.

Before the time came for the Malone family to return to China, Richard had taken a shine to Gladys and

Richard and Gladys Malone (the author's parents) on their wedding day, 2 October 1926

they resolved to keep in touch by letter until they could meet again. In May 1926 the Malones returned to England and on this occasion Richard proposed to Gladys, reputedly beside the pagoda in Kew Gardens. They were married on the 2 October 1926 at St Joseph's church, Highgate – the church where Gladys' parents had been married in 1895. The Malones, together with Gladys, returned to Hankow shortly after the wedding.

Within a few months of her arrival, Gladys was to experience the previously mentioned trip by naval gunboat up the Yangtze with all the other women and children escaping the anti-foreign riots in Hankow. She must have thought what a lawless country she had come to live in, so far from her home in England.

The Next Generation

On 11 June 1928 my sister, Moira Teresa, was born in Hankow General Hospital (delivered by Dr Mainey, a long standing friend of the family). An *amah*, or Chinese nanny, Mae Wha (Lotus Blossom) was employed to look after her. On 27 January 1930, I, Desmond Joseph, was born, also at the Hankow General Hospital and again delivered by Dr Mainey. Amah now had two children to keep her busy.

In this narrative I shall be referring to my father and mother from time to time. When Moira and I were young we always called our parents Mummy and Pappy. As we grew to teenagers and young adults we started to call them Ma and Pop respectively. As I tell my story I shall use Ma and Pop when referring to my parents.

Our amah became a large part of our daily life. She came to be looked on as one of the family. She slept in our part of the house away from the servants' quarters with her husband, a pleasant man many years older than Amah, who had been, at one time, our grandfather's gardener. He did nothing much all day but sit around smoking his water-pipe and smiling pleasantly at us when we were about. Amah was a neat and tidy little woman and always had an aroma of soap and powder about her. She had jet-black hair which was combed straight back off her face without a parting and ending in a neat bun at the nape of her neck. She always wore a short blue jacket and black trousers. When she was born it was the custom for Chinese girl babies to have their feet bound to prevent them growing. Amah had tiny black shoes for her little feet, rather like slippers and made of strong cotton material with cloth soles. She always seemed to have good control over Moira and me. When we got a bit out of hand she had an infallible way of making us behave; she would threaten to leave. The bottom would have fallen out of our world if this had happened. Amah came from Wuchang, immediately opposite Hankow on the south bank of the Yangtze River, which was a mile wide at this point.

Our first home was in Wangpei Road, Hankow. Besides my parents and my sister Moira, Pop's two sisters, Agnes and Maudie lived there as well. In addition, the next generation of our grandparents' servants were now working for us and lived on the premises in the servants' quarters. I have faint recollections of this house. One thing I do remember, however, was that the road opposite was closed by heavy gates every evening. It was a private thoroughfare and only residents of the road could use it after dark. It was called Lockeby Road and I thought, not unreasonably as a small child, that the name had something to do with the closing of the gates!

Moira and I went to St Mary's convent, a school run by an Italian order of nuns – the Connosians. I

The Malone family on holiday in Kuling, 1935

remember, with some dread, Mother Zeta who ran the kindergarten. She had a hard, deeply lined face, a very stern expression and a vicious look in her eye. She wielded a ruler in the classroom and would bring it down with great force on the knuckles of a poor unsuspecting child who was deemed to be misbehaving. I thought she was there to torture little children into learning. The next class was like moving into heaven. Mother Anneta was a beautiful young nun with gentle manners and a wonderful way with children. We all loved her and thought she was an angel who had come down to rescue us from the purgatory we had experienced the year before.

When I was about five-years-old we moved from Wangpei Road to a flat in Sassoon Building on the Bund. We lived there for about two years. It was during this period in my life that I learnt to tell the time. I used to look over the veranda to the Customs House clock a little way down the Bund and call out to whoever cared to listen – the big hand is on the six and the small hand is on the three – what's the time? In this way I eventually learnt to find the answer to the time myself.

Hankow was very hot and oppressive in the summer – the temperature reaching over one hundred degrees Fahrenheit in the shade and Ma, Moira and I, along with most of the European mothers and children, would spend the whole summer in the mountains of Kuling. This resort was south-east of Hankow in the Kiangsi province. The journey to the mountain, was always very exciting. We took a river steamer to Kiukiang. From there we would be transported to the top by wicker chairs, modelled on the lines of the old sedan chair with the exception that they were not closed in. For children, there were two seats facing each other with a tray between them. Each chair was borne by four men with two runners, one either side, who relieved the bearers from time to time. There were several stops on the way up so that these bearers could rest and refresh themselves. After some hours we reached our destination.

We always enjoyed our holidays in Kuling. We met our little friends again and played in the streams and in the rock pools. We had a wonderful time. However, one or two memories were not so pleasant. The owner of the resort kept geese. One day I was standing near them. Perhaps I startled them, but they suddenly moved purposefully in my direction with their heads low on the ground, looking menacing. I decided the best thing for me was to turn tail and run for my life. As I ran, I could hear them lumbering behind me, hissing as they came. The six large birds were determined to get me. Down the hill I ran. Our chalet was in sight and the front door was open. With a last big effort I reached my haven, through the door I went; I slammed it behind me. Looking out of the window, there they were, those geese, baffled and beaten. Although I wouldn't have been more than five years old, possibly younger, that experience has stayed with me all my life.

Another uncomfortable experience I remember was the arrival of the medical team who were there to inoculate all the children. I knew this meant sticking a needle into me and I wanted to escape that if I possibly could. When they arrived at our chalet, I had disappeared. I had hidden myself behind a wardrobe in my parents' room, hoping the team would pass us by and I would escape. No such luck. I was quickly found by Ma when she noticed two small feet behind her wardrobe. No coaxing would entice me out. The wardrobe had to be pulled aside before I could be led from my hiding place. I felt like a lamb to the slaughter. The prick in my arm was over in no time and even I wondered what I had made all the fuss about.

It was Pop's habit to spend the last week of the summer holiday with us and then take us all home to Hankow early in September. This summer expedition to Kuling took place each year up to and including 1935. The following year we went on our first seaside holiday and our first sea trip took us up the coast of China to Tsingtao, the popular seaside resort in Shantung Province in North China – Moira and I had a great time on the lovely sandy beach by the sea. It was an exciting change from our normal holiday plans. However, we shall see later on in this account how the choice of North China a second time, for our holiday in 1937, disrupted our family life more than we could possibly have imagined.

Thinking about our life in Hankow, one early memory I had was when Pop was with the Peking

Hankow Railway. Besides his foreign colleagues, who were French, there were many Chinese on the staff. One Chinese gentleman who did business with Pop at home made a great impression on Moira and me. He was rather elderly, tall for a Chinese man and slim. He had long, slender graceful hands and a finely boned face. He was very dignified. He didn't take any notice of us as we stood in the hall on his arrival. He swept past us and made his way to Pop's study. He was always neatly dressed in his Chinese robes. There was a long blue gown, which fell to his feet. Over this gown he wore a black jacket, rather like a waistcoat. This item of clothing was partly covered by his neatly combed long grey beard. On his head he wore a tiny black scull cap with a little red button on top – a usual headdress for a well-turned-out Chinese gentleman. He looked a rather mysterious figure, perhaps a Chinese Merlin. We nicknamed him Mr Whodze, the Chinese for beard. Pop explained that he was a *comprador*. Such a person was a Chinese manager of a foreign firm in China, acting as a middleman between the foreign business and the Chinese businessmen with whom the firm had dealings.

During our years in Hankow, it seemed to me that all the adult members of the family were always very busy in their different occupations. While Pop was working long hours on the railway, six days a week, Ma taught English at the convent. The teaching of English was a hard slog. Many of the children in the school were Chinese and their English was not good.

Ma spent many hours correcting their homework and conscientiously rewriting her pupils' essays, trying to show them how English should be written. She claimed she wrecked her eyesight during those years doing so many extra hours close work. Auntie Maudie worked full time at the APC and Auntie Aggie taught English and French to adults who came to the house for tuition. Moira and I, when not at school, played together when the adults weren't able to give us their attention. We always had Amah hovering in the background, should her presence be needed.

I remember very clearly our last few years in Hankow up to the summer of 1937 and the fun Moira and I had together. Moira was full of ideas. She invented a village with inhabitants, which she called Nonsensical Land. In this village were the butcher, the baker, the candlestick maker, the doctor, the teacher and most of the other characters you would expect to find in a village. They were all supposed to be a strange bunch and had most extraordinary names: Mr and Mrs Dardelidoo, a person called Gigijaw, another called Ardimardicario. There were two others called Shootinbaby and Norako and many more. Moira drew sketches of all these people and their families. We spent hours making-up stories about them and acting them out. Another aspect of our play was dressing up. Moira had a passion for dressing up, rather dressing me up. I remember in particular the bunny bride, with sheets draped about me. Rabbit ears were made by drawing pieces of sheet through curtain rings to make them stand up. My hands were clasped as in prayer and I put on a sweet face. I played my part well but was glad when it was over. We ran a school for our toys and I enjoyed preparing the exam papers for them. Some of our games, however, didn't always end happily. Two incidents stick in my mind. On one occasion, Moira and I were sitting on the floor of the bathroom which adjoined our parents' bedroom. The game was to try and kick the other while in the sitting position. This entailed a certain amount of lunging about. Moira eased herself forward to bring her foot down on my leg. Seeing what was about to happen I jumped backwards and through the glass-panelled door of the bathroom. The glass shattered everywhere and showered down upon me. Miraculously, I emerged unscathed. Moira was very worried. She knew she would get into trouble for leading her little brother astray. Another exciting exploit ended in blood and tears. There was a very large wardrobe in our parents' room. Moira conceived the idea that it would be great fun if we swung on the wardrobe doors. Each of us took a door and began to swing. It soon became apparent, certainly to Moira if not to me, that our combined weight was too much for the wardrobe. It wobbled uncertainly and then crashed to the ground. Moira saw what was happening and jumped clear. I was not so perceptive and found myself under the heavy piece of furniture, where a sharp metal drawer handle had ripped a deep slice in my chin. Moira saw me lying there, pouring with blood. In panic she ran from the room, down the stairs two at a time and burst into the parlour where Auntie Aggie was teaching English to a foreign gentleman. 'Come quickly Auntie, come quickly,' she shouted, 'Desmond's dead.' Auntie Aggie rose from her chair in a calm and well-contained manner. 'Will you please excuse me, Mr Frangakis,' she said, leaving the room. Upstairs it looked as if a tornado had ripped through the room. The wardrobe was spreadeagled on the floor with its doors forced out on either side, and the drawers at the bottom were partially pulled out and jammed. There was a large blob of blood on the floor and tell-tale drops which led to a chair in the corner of the room where Amah was sitting with me on her lap. Her hand was cupped under my chin, which was still bleeding, and she was wailing 'Desamun die or; Desamun die or'. There was nothing for it but to get me to hospital as quickly as possible. While I was being stitched up in hospital, Moira was once again getting into big trouble. The scar on my chin is visible to this day. I can only think that Amah was not aware of our latest antic, otherwise she surely would have nipped it in the bud before anything happened.

Although Moira and I played together for hours quite happily, we also had our fair share of parties. Going to gatherings was not my favourite pastime, but I put up with them as I was expected to go. However, on one occasion I was invited to the birthday party of a little girl in my class whom I described as 'the girl who sits behind my seat'. Amah took me along to my friend's house. The mother of my little hostess took me into the room where the party was about to start. To my horror, as I looked around, there wasn't a boy in sight. I'm afraid this was not for me. I escaped without being noticed and was out in the road in no time. I ran as fast as I could all the way home. Ma was astonished to see me. 'What are you doing here, you are supposed to be at the party?' she said, 'Where's Amah?' All was explained to her. When Amah arrived back she was visibly shocked to see me at home. Ma explained what had happened and told Amah not to worry, she was not to blame for what I had done. Ma was left with the embarrassing task of having to apologise for my behaviour.

In 1937 my parents decided that we should try another seaside resort in the summer as the Tsingtao holiday had been such a success. They chose Peitahao, a second town on the North China coast in Hopeh Province where there were good sandy beaches. To add to the interest of the holiday we would stop at Peking on the way. This was the ancient capital city of China. While there, we would be able to visit the Forbidden City, that part of Peking where the emperor and his court resided in imperial days, that is, before 1911. To go to Peking and then on to Peitahao we, as children, were to experience our first train trip. Before we left I said to Amah in an unthinking and insensitive way, 'I don't ever want to come back to Hankow again.' Amah was alarmed.

'Don't say such things,' she said, 'the wicked spirits

will hear you and will make sure you never come back again.' I smiled, unconvinced. As you will see from the narrative which follows, we weren't able to return to Hankow at the end of our holiday and we didn't ever see Amah again. I am sure she must have thought that my remark had been picked up by those sharp-eared wicked spirits and they had decided to prevent our return to Hankow.

We left for our holiday shortly after the middle of June. In Peking we stayed in an hotel owned by an American woman married to a Chinese gentleman. It was a lovely place and had at one time been a traditional wealthy Chinese home. The main building, which would originally have been where the head of the family lived, was the dining hall. The rest of the houses were built in a circle round a courtyard and in days gone by would have been where the sons of the family lived. These houses were now for the guests. Visiting the Forbidden City was a most exciting experience. We saw Peking in her ancient glory. No foreign influence there, totally Chinese in style. Coloured roof tiles, red arches, white stone with stunning carvings. I remember visiting the Temple of Heaven and Temple of the Goddess of Mercy. We took in all the sights and were impressed with all we saw. After this exciting few days we went to Peitahao to carry on our holiday. There were lovely sandy beaches. Moira seemed to enjoy burying me in the sand with just my head and hands showing. I was always a compliant playmate. Moira and I enjoyed riding donkeys on the beach. It was another experience we hadn't previously had. After many days enjoying ourselves, Pop received instructions to return to Hankow without delay. It seems an incident had occurred in the suburbs of Peking on the 7 July between Japanese and Chinese troops and it looked as if it might develop into something more serious. As he left for Hankow on the 15 July, Pop said we were to stay where we were until the situation eased and then try to return home to Hankow.

The Build-up to China's War with Japan

Chiang Kai-shek's success against the warlords in 1926 so alarmed Borodin, the Russian chief representative for directing the Chinese Communists, that he was determined to disrupt the Nationalist army's achievements.

The last thing he wanted was for the Nationalist government to take credit for uniting the country. In Nanking and Shanghai, the Communists sought to engineer uprisings to provoke clashes between the foreign powers and Chiang's revolutionary forces. More evidence of Communist subversion and treason were reported to the Kuomintang Central Supervisory Committee in April 1927. Reports continued to be received where the Chinese Communists, on orders from the Communist International, were orchestrating disturbances to sabotage the Nationalist revolution and to disrupt social order. So severe had the disruption by the Communists become, following the dictates of their Soviet masters, that the National Government (Kuomintang) in December 1927 severed its diplomatic relations with Russia and ordered the closure of all Russian diplomatic missions and business establishments in China. Before the diplomatic break with Soviet Russia, the National Government had purged all Communists from the army and the government. By 1930, with the warlords no longer an important issue, Chiang was able to devote his energies to defeating the Communists in the field. It took five campaigns to complete the task. The Nationalists first drove the Communists from China's southern provinces and then pursued them north of the Yangtze river where they were routed. The Communists scattered and made their way north until they reached the northern province of Shensi. By early 1935 their forces were reduced to a mere 5,000 armed men, so they surrendered, asking for the cessation of hostilities.

These resolute actions by Chiang both on the political and military front effectively delayed Communist control of the Chinese mainland until some years after the Second World War. However, the Communists still remained a thorn in the side for Chiang. In 1935 they tried to save themselves by political means in calling for a united front to resist Japanese aggression, which was becoming more threatening as the years progressed. A Communist directed 'people's front' emerged, which sought to undermine the loyalty of Chiang's troops and prevent them from taking any action against the Communists – 'Fight Japan and not the Communists' and 'Chinese must not fight Chinese' were the slogans.

In 1937, before satisfactorily dealing with the Communist menace once and for all, a greater and more urgent need faced Chiang – a direct challenge from Japan.

As mentioned earlier in this narrative, Japan had an aggressive expansionist policy towards China. To reiterate the chain of events: in 1894 Japan acquired Formosa after the war with China and was able to remove China's overlordship of Korea.

In the Russian–Japanese War of 1904/5, Japan defeated Imperial Russia and removed Russian influence from Korea and Manchuria. Korea was made part of the Japanese empire in 1910. In Manchuria, Japan gained control of the South Manchurian Railway. Her next major objective was to acquire the whole of Manchuria with its rich fertile soil, its forests and its minerals. This would provide a stepping stone to more conquests in China itself. She bided her time and watched events.

At the outbreak of the Great War of 1914–1918, Japan declared war on Germany and seized the German Concessions in the northern province of Shantung. In 1919, against China's wishes, Japan was formally granted all Germany's Chinese territory by the post-war peace settlement. There was violent reaction to this by China. The German Concessions were eventually returned to China as an outcome of the Washington Conference of 1921/22. However, when Chiang's Nationalist Army reached Shantung Province in 1928, on its expedition to recapture warlord territory, the Japanese reacted. Though German Concessions had been returned to China, Japanese residence in Shantung had increased dramatically and the area was still considered to 'belong' to Japan. The Japanese reaction took place in the town of Tsinan. The outcome was that 7,000 Chinese were killed. Japan wreaked this carnage by bringing in numbers of troops to defend 'their province' against invasion. In September 1931, Japan marched into Manchuria. They consolidated their position by renaming it Manchukuo, setting it up as a puppet state and chose Pu-Yi, the last emperor of the Manchu dynasty, to be its ruler. Chinese riots followed in Nanking and Shanghai over Japanese moves in Manchuria. In January 1932, to assert her authority again on the Chinese mainland, ostensibly to protect her own citizens, Japan sent her marines into Shanghai and entered the Chapei district where many Japanese civilians lived. For two months Japan pounded the area, leaving 35,000 Chinese and Japanese soldiers, plus Chinese civilians, dead.

In spite of all this, for the next four years, ignoring such blatant aggression and unabashed Japanese terror tactics together with frequent infringements of Chinese territory, Chiang Kai-shek, as we have seen, continued to concentrate all the efforts of the Nationalist government and its army on the destruction of the Communist party in his country. Strong feelings in some Nationalists developed, encouraged by the Communists, that Chiang should have been more aggressive, at a time like this, against Japan, rather than expending his energy on defeating other Chinese. He was taken prisoner in December 1936 in Sian by certain of the Commanders of Government troops working with the Communists. His captors demanded of Chiang that he should present a united front against Japan. Chou En-lai, the leading Communist, was the mediator. An agreement was struck between government forces and the Communists after lengthy discussions and a united front, at least on paper, was formed to face the common enemy.

The Sino–Japanese War

On 7 July 1937, while Japanese troops were on night manoeuvres near the Marco Polo Bridge a few miles outside Peking, they had an accidental confrontation with a Chinese patrol which led to casualties on both sides. This was the incident which prompted Pop's recall to Hankow from our holiday in Peitahao that summer. Little did he know that this was something much more serious. In fact, the incident provoked Japan into launching an all-out invasion of North China. This was the start of the Sino–Japanese war.

By the end of July, Japanese forces had taken Peking and Tientsin, the chief cities in the North. Fortunately, foreign residents were not threatened at this time as the war was not directed against them. By August there was fierce fighting in the centre of Shanghai. A long stretch of Nanking Road, a leading thoroughfare in that city, was almost carpeted with the dead. Battles over the city were fought between Japanese and Chinese bombers, anti-aircraft guns and naval guns. The well-known department store Wing-on was hit by a bomb, causing great loss of life.

Not long before our family had left for our holiday in 1937, Auntie Maudie had been posted by the APC to Shanghai. She and Auntie Aggie found a very comfortable boarding house called The Villas in the

French Concession in Avenue Foch, run by a Scottish lady, Mrs Fisher. In that August, when all the fighting was going on in the streets of Shanghai, Auntie Maudie continued to travel daily to her work at the APC in the heart of the business area. Bodies could be seen stacked high on both sides of the road as the fighting continued. It must have been a harrowing experience for her each day. However, in spite of the mayhem, foreign residents in Shanghai, as in Peking and Tientsin, unless hit by accident, were generally not harmed. As they occupied the city, the Japanese did not enter the foreign areas, that is, the International Settlement and the French Concession.

In December, the enemy's advance deep into China continued. They overwhelmed the important town of Nanking, which Chiang's government had made the national capital in April 1927 to fulfil Dr Sun's wishes. The Chinese inhabitants there suffered the worst atrocities of the Sino–Japanese war. This was not just war, this was human savagery beyond the bounds of imagination. Nanking experienced a storm of violence and cruelty that has few parallels. Female rape victims, many of whom died after repeated assaults, were estimated at 2,000; fugitive Chinese soldiers killed numbered approximately 30,000; murdered civilians, 12,000. Robbery, wanton destruction and arson left much of the city in ruins. This barbaric treatment by Japan of the Chinese people in that city has gone down in history as the Rape of Nanking; a stark example of man's inhumanity to man. One extraordinary fact about all this was that the foreigners, cocooned in their own areas, continued their own Western way of life and seemed oblivious to the terrible suffering and carnage wreaked on the Chinese people by Japan, not only in Nanking but elsewhere in China. This attitude was illustrated by the way many Western residents of China were far more outraged over the Japanese bombing of the American gunboat USS *Panay*, taking refugees from Nanking, than the horrific brutality that the Chinese had suffered in that city. As the Chinese forces were driven southward, Chiang's Nationalist army burst dykes or set fire to cities before abandoning them to the Japanese. In October 1938, the city of Canton in South China was set on fire by retreating Nationalists. As the Japanese moved relentlessly through China, Chiang retreated to Chungking, a city on the Yangtze River deep in the western province of Szechwan. It became China's wartime capital in December 1938. Following their army, Chinese refugees from Eastern China began to fill Chungking. The British Ambassador, Sir Archibald Clerk-Kerr, moved his embassy there also. At this time, in late 1938 and in 1939, the flood of Jewish refugees fleeing Nazi Germany was increasing rapidly. These refugees who had been coming since 1933 to Shanghai reached 10,000 by June 1939. The Japanese designated a ghetto for them in the run-down district of Hong Kew. The Jews were no strangers to Shanghai. Famous Jewish families had lived there for years. Sassoon, Kadoorie and Hardoon were household names.

When the war between China and Japan started in July 1937, Ma, Moira and I were enjoying our seaside holiday in Peitahao. Pop, as previously mentioned, returned to our home in Hankow a few days after the July incident. As there was no immediate prospect of our returning to Hankow to join him, we made our way to Tientsin, with the intention of trying to get home when safe to do so. With financial help from the British Consul we were put up in the States Hotel. We stayed in Tientsin for about three and a half months. I started school there in September at St Louis, run by the Marist Brothers, a French order. Moira went to the Sacred Heart convent. After only two weeks at the school I implored my mother to take me away, I hated it. I joined Moira at the convent. I remember taking my place in the queue of children filing off to their classrooms with a feeling of sheer bliss. No rough horrible little boys, just gentle orderly girls (and a rare boy or two), with kindly nuns looking after us.

Letters from Pop began to trickle through to Tientsin from Hankow. He was very lonely and anxious for our return, with only our two pets, Tippy, Ma's white cat, and Wuzu, our family dog, to keep him company.

While in Tientsin, Ma was very worried and her nerves were on edge. Any undue naughtiness from Moira or myself was a great strain on her. One afternoon we were having a siesta on our beds in the hotel. I wasn't feeling particularly tired and, to while away the time, I carved my name on the wall beside me. I

Moira and Desmond, aged ten and eight years old, 1938

thought nothing of it. When Ma discovered what I had done she collapsed in a chair and burst into tears. Moira and I were shocked and rushed to comfort her. Normally, she was very self-contained and didn't show her emotions. We thought there must be something seriously wrong. 'You naughty children,' she said, scolding both of us for my misdeed. 'How can you go on like this? Here we are stuck in this hotel, in a strange city, with no money. They will charge us for the damage to the wall. We can't even pretend it doesn't have anything to do with us as your name gives us away,' she said, looking hard at me. As it happened, Ma needn't have worried. We heard nothing; it probably wasn't even noticed by the hotel staff.

By the middle of November 1937 there didn't seem to be the remotest chance of being able to return to Hankow and, since domestic shipping had just been resumed down the coast of China, Ma resolved to go south to Shanghai and join the aunties there. We travelled on the SS *Tai Yuen* of Jardine Matheson, one of the leading British shipping companies operating in China. We were met by Pop's sisters, who were overjoyed to see us. They took us to The Villas where they were living. We were also able to be accommodated by Mrs Fisher. Uncle George and his Russian wife, Nina, were living not too far away. We settled in quite comfortably. Moira went to the Sacred Heart convent and I started my schooling at the Marist Brothers school, St Jeanne D'Arc College in Rue de Gruchy. I joined the altar boys in 1938, trained by

Brother Blazius, a stickler for perfection. I learnt the art of serving Mass, from him, and the Latin responses, at my mother's knee. She put me through my paces until I was word perfect. Her thoroughness gave rise to a compliment on her teaching when she was told years later how well and clearly I pronounced the Latin. In fact, I learnt a great deal at that school under the guiding hand and swishing cane of Brother Kevin from Kilkenny.

It was late in 1937 or early 1938 that Moira and I started piano lessons in Rue de Gruchy with Mr Steiner, a white Russian Jew, who claimed to be the pupil of the pupil of the Russian composer Rubenstein. Mr Steiner had escaped the Bolshevik revolution of 1917 and had made his way to China like so many of his kinsmen. A bust of Rubenstein stood in his piano room. During the lessons he would walk up and down the room drawing heavily on his cigarette, shaking his head in disapproval and flicking his cigarette ash all over the room in a distracted way. He expected us to practise the piano for two hours every day and he was never satisfied with our performances – particularly mine. He was appalled that he, the pupil of the pupil of Rubinstein, should have to listen to such incompetence on the keyboard.

As our life in Shanghai became more normal, Pop, who had returned to Hankow in July 1937 from Peitahao, soon realised that his days with the railway were numbered. He was still employed by the middle of 1938 but, as his activities were considerably curtailed, he was receiving only a small proportion of the pay which would have been due to him in normal circumstances. He was finally dismissed from his job in which he had worked for nearly forty years. Pop claimed to be the last foreigner to leave the Peking Hankow Railway. He left his employment with no pension, no redundancy pay nor any other form of remuneration to send him on his way. Luckily, within a matter of a week or two he was able to obtain employment with Jardine Matheson on one of their ships, the SS *Kiang Wo* as the Purser. He took up his appointment on the 25 July 1938. In normal times the *Kiang Wo* would sail up and down the Yangtze between Hankow and Shanghai, but this stretch of the river had been closed to normal traffic by the Japanese. However, the ship gave a restricted service between Hankow and Ichang, a town a few hundred miles further up the river. In fact, the travel between the two towns was very spasmodic and during his time with the ship, Pop found he was generally berthed in Ichang.

After joining the *Kiang Wo* and having no settled home, Pop arranged for our two animals to be found temporary homes. Tippy, Ma's white cat was passed over to Mother Cecilia, the headmistress of our Hankow convent, to look after until we were able to have her back. Wuzu, our little dog, went to a lady some distance up the Yangtze at Shasi. Amah was still living in Sassoon Building, helping a Chinese gentleman who had taken over our flat while we were all away. Amah's hope was that we would return to Hankow one day and she would be able to live with us again.

We were lucky enough to be able to communicate with Pop by letter, but these took a fortnight to reach him. However, Ma was able to send a radio message to him every Saturday through the good offices of Jardines, who allowed wives of officers on the ships in Hankow and Ichang to communicate with their husbands in this way.

As the Sino–Japanese war began in 1937, the Chinese Communists were shortly to be seen in their true colours. In the autumn of 1937, the leading Communist, Mao Tse-Tung, addressing his troops, said the war with Japan gave them, the Chinese Communists, an excellent opportunity for expansion. Their policy was to devote seventy per cent of their efforts towards their own expansion, twenty per cent to coping with the Nationalist Government and ten per cent to fighting the Japanese. With no significant role to play in resisting the enemy, Communist guerrillas established themselves in areas abandoned by the Japanese and the Nationalist troops. Pop told us a story about one activity that a group of Communist guerrillas had engaged in. An Italian Catholic mission-ary priest, Father Epifanio, a fine figure of a man, standing 6' 6" in his stocking feet, was kidnapped by these guerrillas and taken to an old wooden hut for 'interrogation' in a remote part of the Chinese hinter-land. The interior of the hut was bare except for a rough wooden table and two chairs standing on plain floorboards. The only adornment was a framed picture of Stalin on the wall. The priest was directed to one of the chairs at the table and the chief interrogator sat opposite him. The rest of the group stood around listening. The interrogation proceeded for some time but didn't seem to be going very smoothly. Exasperated, the interrogator pointed to the picture on the wall. 'Who is that?' he shouted. Father Epifanio examined it very carefully and shook his head. 'Who is that person?' the interrogator persisted.

The priest looked again and replied, 'I don't know who he is but I can see that, like me, he is a foreign devil.' His onlookers immediately saw the funny side of it and fell about the room in uncontrolled laughter. The priest was released shortly afterwards.

Good news was to arrive from Ichang very shortly. Early in 1939 Jardine's Shanghai office decided Pop should leave the *Kiang Wo* and come down to Shanghai. Since the Yangtze was blocked east of Hankow, he had to adopt a circuitous route to undertake the journey. He needed to travel from Ichang, westward up the Yangtze River for 350 miles through the gorges to Chunking. From there he flew on the 10 March to Hanoi in French Indo–China (now Vietnam). At Hanoi, with one and a half hours to spare, he was required to join the Jardine's ship the SS *Taksang* berthed at Haiphong, on the coast, which was leaving at 6 p.m. that evening for Hong Kong. There wouldn't be another ship for a week if he missed that one. The next train from Hanoi to Haiphong would not arrive in Haiphong until 8 p.m. that evening, which was too late. Pop and an American gentleman, Captain Sutherland, who was also anxious to get to Hong Kong, decided to hire a car and race to Haiphong. They arrived at 6.30 p.m. having travelled at top speed the whole way. Driving down to the quay, they found to their relief the *Taksang* still berthed there. It appeared that the delay in the ship's departure was that it had a great deal of cargo to stow in its hold. The ship eventually set sail for Hong Kong at 10 p.m. that night, and happily, with Pop safely on board. They arrived in Hong Kong on the 13 March.

Early on 15 March, Pop left for Shanghai on another of Jardine's ships, the SS *Ting Sang* for the last leg of his journey and arrived without mishap on the 19 March. Although we had been able to get in touch with him in Hankow and Ichang, it had been twenty months since we had seen him after he left Peitahao in July 1937. It was a great reunion, but not complete. Moira and Auntie Maudie were in England.

Moira Visits England

In 1938 Auntie Maudie was due for her home leave. On this occasion she took Moira with her. They were booked on the German ship, the *Scharnhaust*, of the Norddeucher Lloyd line of Bremen. Their voyage was to start just before Christmas. When the day arrived, Ma and I went to see them off on their long journey to England. Before we arrived at the wharf I was told I would be excited to see a very large ocean liner. However, I caused some embarrassment when on board. After looking around for a short while I said in a loud voice, 'This isn't a very big ship.' The first officer standing nearby to welcome the travellers on board was not amused. He looked most annoyed that this young boy should so disparage his pride and joy. He distanced himself from us to pay his attention to the more appreciative passengers.

As the ship pulled out from Shanghai, Moira, a mere ten years old, who had never before left home or her mother, felt rather miserable. This feeling soon left her as they got underway and she was absorbed in her surroundings. On the journey they stopped at Hong Kong, where they had a very enjoyable day at Repulse Bay, the most popular beach on the island. They spent the morning on the beach and then had 'tiffin' at the Repulse Bay Hotel, having a splendid meal there. They returned to the beach in the afternoon to collect shells and afterwards made their way to the Hong Kong Hotel for tea. They then caught the ferry back to the ship. They stopped at Manila, Borneo, Singapore and Penang, going ashore to see the sights. At their next port of call, Columbo, Moira bought a large black wooden elephant for Ma – it was a most handsome ornament. It still graces the shelves of the family. After Port Said and Aden they reached the Italian city of Genoa. There Moira was entertained by the goolie goolie man who performed magic in front of her and pulled little chicks out of her ears. She was most impressed. They finally arrived at Southampton twenty-seven days after leaving Shanghai. It was a wonderful voyage which included celebrating Christmas on board, and proved a most exciting occasion.

When they arrived in England, Moira and Auntie Maudie were invited to stay with Beryl and Cecil Fitt, one of Ma's younger sisters and her husband at Timberscombe, their home in New Malden, Surrey. They stayed with the Fitts for about two months and Moira got to know their daughter Deirdre, aged seven years, very well and also her younger sister Jennifer, who was two years old. While staying at Timberscombe, Moira had the opportunity of meeting the other members of the family. Living nearby in New Malden was Emily O'Donnell (Granny) and Maudie, Ma's second sister who was unmarried and living at home; Desmond, Ma's brother, and his wife Chrissie who lived at Chalk Farm in North London;

Also in North London, in Muswell Hill, were Cecile, the youngest sister in the O'Donnell family and Dermot Kilgallin, her husband, with their children, Kevin who was two years and Claire, a few months old. In March 1939 our travellers went to Ireland for a month with the main object of giving Moira the chance of visiting, for the first time, a number of relatives there. They first stopped in Dublin where they met Uncle Jim O'Donnell (Ma's uncle) living his bachelor life in that city. They then travelled to the west of Ireland to Castlebar, Co. Mayo, to stay with Pop's two aunts, Mrs Annie Miller and Miss Katie Cosgrove. Auntie Annie was well into her eighties and Katie in her late sixties. Moira and Auntie Maudie spent most of the time meeting the 'town' and had a very enjoyable stay. They then went down to Limerick City to meet the rest of the O'Donnell family and stayed with Uncle Jim's unmarried sisters, Chrissie, Mary Kate and Emile. From this base they visited the O'Connors, Muhollands and two other O'Donnell houses. After this whirlwind round of visiting relatives, our travellers returned to England and stayed with Granny and Maudie in New Malden.

All the time Moira was in England she kept in close touch with us by letter and Ma wrote to her practically every week, keeping her up to date on the China scene. Moira was pleased to hear that Pop, who had been stranded in Ichang for so long, was due to arrive in Shanghai in March 1939. Ma in her letters expressed the hope that we might still be able to return to

Hankow when the Yangtze River was opened up for normal travel again. Some of our friends were filtering back there, notwithstanding the travel difficulties. Moira also heard that our close friends the Farrells and their two daughters Kathleen and Colleen were living in Canton in South China.

Moira and Auntie Maudie left England in June for the return journey home. They made their way to Rotterdam in Holland to join the *Bergenland*, another German ship, to take them back to China. They returned by the same route. There was a tense atmosphere on board, where most of the passengers were Jews leaving Nazi Germany for a better life elsewhere. Moira heard many disturbing stories from her newfound young German Jewish friends about life in Germany for the Jewish people. None of us could have had the remotest idea at this time, when we in China heard these stories, to what depths of fiendish activity this diabolical Nazi regime could sink. They had no lesser goal than the extermination of the Jewish race itself in countries under their jackboot.

My sister and our aunt were the only British passengers on board. Their ship arrived in Shanghai on the 24 of July to a great welcome from us all.

A Trip to Haiphong

As we have seen, Pop arrived in Shanghai from Ichang in March 1939. He was soon assigned to a new ship, the SS *Taisunghong*. After some ten days or so in Shanghai with us he joined his ship in Hong Kong. She was a vessel chartered by Jardines and travelled up the coast of China – north to Tientsin and south to Haiphong in French Indo–China (now Vietnam). When Moira and Auntie Maudie arrived back from England in July, Pop was away and didn't return to Shanghai for about another week. When they met, it was two years since Pop and Moira had last seen each other. This was a short-lived reunion because within about three days Ma and I joined Pop for a trip to Haiphong via Hong Kong. We set off at the beginning of August. Ma and I shared a cabin next door to Pop's, who had the purser's quarters. The whole ship had a strong French flavour about it. The captain was a Frenchman, as were his first and second officers. Pop, the purser, was as good as a Frenchman, having been on the railway with the French for most of his working life, and spoke as fluently as they did. The rest of the crew were Anamites, or natives of French Indo–China, and their second language was French, which they always used on board. If any further evidence of a French flavour to the ship were needed, it was provided by Captain Courcer himself. He exuded an all pervading aroma of wine which moved with him wherever he went. He was a cheerful middle-aged man and very entertaining company.

Not more than a day or so after the start of our holiday on board we heard a wireless news item which reported that the *Kiang Wo*, the ship Pop had left earlier in the year, had been bombed in Ichang by the Japanese and had been completely destroyed. It was a sad moment for him.

We arrived in Hong Kong on the morning of the 10 August and spent three or four days there. This gave us an opportunity to have a look at the island. The one event which sticks in my mind was a midnight feast we had on the beach at Repulse Bay, one of the most attractive stretches of sand and sea on the island. Captain Courcer, Pop, Ma and I had great fun there on the beach. The captain was in party mood. He put his feet on the picnic table and turned to me and said, 'We are here to enjoy ourselves. We can do anything we like on a picnic.' It was good fun with this rather showy and, at party times, generally inebriated Frenchman.

After Hong Kong our journey down the coast of China continued. I felt a very important nine-year-old when I was taken on a personal tour of the ship by the first officer. I went up on the bridge, a most exciting experience. He told me how the ship was navigated and promised to show me the sky by night and the stars in their constellations and how ships could still use the stars to ensure they were on a correct course. We looked around the decks and finally the officer took me down to the engine room to see and have explained to me the great power that was needed to drive the ship along.

After a few days we arrived in Haiphong, a port in French Indo–China where the ship remained for some nine days, if my memory serves me correctly. Ma and I went ashore each day to see the town. What struck me more than anything else was how all the people seemed to enjoy chewing betel nut and squirting the juice out of their mouths so that the pavements were streaked in red everywhere. This chewing practice seemed to give them black tongues – a most strange habit. I liked wandering around the town and seeing the sights and I am sure Ma did also, especially looking at the shops and buying novel items that caught her eye. We returned to Shanghai via Hong Kong, where we stopped briefly before the last leg of our journey home. I enjoyed the holiday very much. Ma found it a restful trip and a good opportunity for her to be with Pop for a whole month after their two years' separation. We arrived back in Shanghai early in September. The Second World War had begun.

The war at that time was being fought in Europe and had little effect then on our lives in the Far East. Ma was, of course, worried for her family in England but there was nothing that she could do to help. In our part of the world, the war between China and Japan had been going on since July 1937. It had undoubtedly disrupted our lives and had caused Ma, in particular, a great deal of heartache but, as foreigners, we had thankfully escaped physical danger. Japan's brutal but successful campaign in China found that by 1940 she had gained possession of seven of China's largest cities: Peking, Tientsin, Tsingtao, Nanking, Hankow, Shanghai and Canton. She also held all China's major ports. From 1940–1945, Nanking was the seat of the Chinese puppet government, nominally under President Wang Ching-wei, who had been appointed by the Japanese as early as 1937. Wang was a man who put his own life and career first, and any patriotic feeling for his country came a poor second. He had demonstrated this approach to life with the arrival of the Soviet Communists in the 1920s. He had aligned himself with the Communists as a better bet than helping Chiang Kai-shek to unite the country and rid China of the Communist canker. The Nationalists regarded Wang as a traitor to his country. The Japanese could see from the start that he would be putty in their hands and was the obvious choice to head the puppet government.

By the time we returned from our holiday on the *Taisunghong* in early September, school had restarted. I threw myself into the activities of the new term. I used to travel from The Villas in Avenue Foch to my school in Rue de Gruchy. I went by rickshaw: a light two-wheeled hooded vehicle pulled by a running rickshaw coolie holding two long shafts protruding in front of the vehicle. The passenger sat on a cushion on the seat under the rickshaw's hood. Unless one had a car, it was probably the most usual form of transport used by foreigners to travel from one part of a Chinese city to another. A gnarled little rickshaw coolie got to know when I came out of my house for school in the morning and when I was ready to go home in the afternoon. He was always there with his rickshaw and I was able to use him daily without the slightest worry that he wouldn't turn up. Friends of ours, the Clears, who were living in Shanghai, decided to return to Hankow and I was able to take over their private rickshaw for school, an upmarket version of the basic one I had been using. I was sorry for the little rickshaw man who had been so faithful to me and whom I had abandoned for the sake of a more stylish vehicle.

Life in Canton

Early in 1940, the Canton agent for Jardine Matheson's, a Mr Todd, had left China in the hope of returning to England in spite of the war. His fine black and white English setter named Bob was to be passed on to the next incumbent of the job. That position was taken by Pop. He left Shanghai without delay and arrived in Canton in March 1940. Ma, Moira and I were expected to follow him shortly afterwards. In the event, the Japanese closed the Pearl River to civilian travel and prevented us from joining him by the only route which would have been available to us. It was not until February 1941 that the river was opened again and we were able to leave Shanghai for our new home in Canton. We journeyed south to Hong Kong on the SS *Fausang*. At Hong Kong we met an old friend of the family, Bill O'Neil, who worked for Reuters. He saw us off the following day on our eighty-mile trip up the Pearl River to Canton. For this last stretch of our journey we boarded the Japanese vessel the *Shirogani Maru*, the only available passenger steamer at the time on the Hong Kong–Canton run.

The city of Canton, in normal times, was not frequented by foreigners. With the arrival of the Japanese in 1938 few, if any, foreigners were permitted to enter the city. Most of them lived and worked on Shameen.

This was a man-made island approximately two by four miles on the river front. It was built with concrete, earth and banuan trees, the roots of which were said to hold it together. There was a heavily guarded connecting bridge to the mainland, which was the only entrance to the city from the island. Some foreign residents lived down the river at the installations and compounds belonging to the firms for which they worked.

Most of the Germans lived in the Lutheran mission, which was across the Pearl River, opposite Shameen. All of those who lived down the river had motor boats to take them to and from Shameen which was the focal point for all our activities. Pop met us on arrival. He showed us around the island and Jardine Matheson's main residence, which was at that time unoccupied. It had a great hall in which receptions and other functions were held in more affluent days. We could have lived there had we wished but Ma decided the more modest house down the river would do us very well. Pop then took us by the company's motor boat for our two mile trip to Taichunghao Wharf, the Jardine's residence on the river where he had been living since his arrival in Canton. As we approached we were delighted to see this most attractive property, which was to be our home as long as we were able to stay in Canton. The house was a restful green wooden elevation, surrounded by verandas enclosed by mosquito screens on both floors and topped by a red tiled roof. It was protected from the river by two tall lush

The house in Canton from the Pearl River, 1941

green trees. The front of the property, facing the river, was bordered by a small white-painted fence. The path to the front door divided a garden of ferns and red hibiscus. There was a fairly large garden on the left-hand side of the house, which sported a variety of trees including tall attractive palms and two papaya trees, with succulent papayas which resemble water melons. This juicy sweet orange-coloured fruit, I declared, was the best thing I had tasted in all my life. We had a frangipani tree also, with strange looking branches like antlers. We called it our 'Me-and-my-horns tree'. There was a fine lawn on that side of the house, surrounded by a high brick wall and a small circular lily pond and fountain. It was well stocked with fish. It looked very picturesque on the edge of the lawn. The interior of the house, which was encircled by verandas, had two large reception rooms downstairs and similar-sized bedrooms above. My parents had one of the bedrooms and Moira the other. A corner of the veranda near Pop and Ma's room was turned into a small bedroom for me. Behind the house was a yard with a roofed path that led to the kitchen and servants' quarters. We had a full complement of servants, all of the same family – a cook, houseboy, coolie, a gardener and a wash amah. Adjacent to the house on the water-front was Taichunghao Wharf itself, where Jardine's ships would berth in more normal times. Beyond our walled garden was a disused tennis court, which we were able to use from time to time. The rest of the compound, apart from offices, godowns (warehouses) and buildings that accommodated the remaining staff, were large fields. In the corner of one of them were stables. As Jardine's now had no horses, these stables were let out and at that time housed seven black goats and two ponies. There were many ducks and chickens that also roamed the compound. It was fun for Moira and me to wander around these areas and explore. So far as our own pets were concerned, in addition to Bob, the dog we had inherited from Mr Todd, was a second dog called Rangi who went with the house. Rangi was the outside dog, a mongrel who hadn't been house-trained and was not allowed indoors. Bob was the inside dog as he had been properly brought up. Rangi was very jealous of Bob and they had some ferocious fights. Poor Rangi always got the worst of it as Bob was a bigger and stronger animal. Next door to us lived a customs officer, an elderly man with grey hair and goatee beard. He was a white Russian named Sadkowski. He kept himself very much to himself so we learnt very little about him. He was the only other foreigner living on Jardine's property and must have rented his house from the firm.

The company motor boat was used by us daily to go up to Shameen. It was operated by the *laudah* who was assisted by the boat boy, two very pleasant men. Moira and I travelled up with Pop every morning to school and Pop to his office. On other occasions we used the boat to go up the river to Shameen to the church, the swimming pool or sometimes to stay with friends. Kathleen and Colleen Farrell, children we had grown up with in Hankow and later in Shanghai, had been in Canton with their parents since 1939. We were pleased to see them again.

We soon found that the convent school we attended was far from ideal. There were open-plan classrooms and several school years were housed together in one big room. It was noisy and the teaching left a lot to be desired. Moira stuck it out at the school, but I was taken away and Ma instructed me at home. She was an experienced teacher and had taught in schools in Shanghai and Hankow. Another activity which took up her time was practising her singing. Before she was married Ma had trained for ten years as a singer and had hired a studio in London to practise, not far from where she worked in Wigmore Street. She sang at public events in China and was highly praised for her soprano voice. She was also involved in raising money to support the war effort. Many women arranged bridge or mahjong parties during the day. Ma went for mahjong, a game she enjoyed playing. When at home, supposedly doing my studies, I would see large droves of women descending upon the house to have a pleasant and noisy afternoon playing mahjong. However, being a knitter, Ma's main contribution towards the war effort was to make endless woollen balaclava helmets for the fighting forces.

Moira and I were taught to swim by Mr Farmer, a resident of Shameen, who had a young family. He took it upon himself to teach any new youngsters who arrived at the Shameen swimming pool and wanted to learn to swim. We were lucky enough to make great strides in our swimming and were taken under the wing of a young Danish man, Mr Rasmussen who had been the Hong Kong freestyle champion. He taught us the Australian crawl. Moira, at thirteen, showed great promise and Mr Rasmussen was trying to bring her up to the standard required to enter the women's freestyle championships in Hong Kong the following year. We became very friendly with Mr Rasmussen and met his young wife Norma. Moira and I were taken out on a few occasions on the river in his rowing boat or on his yacht and we started to learn the rudiments of rowing and sailing. The one alarming part of our exploits on the river was the regular appearance, on her scheduled journey, of the Japanese ship the *Shirogani Maru*, which thundered up the Pearl River, swamping small craft as it went. We survived the ordeal by pointing our bow at the oncoming waves and rode them with ease. This was the ship that had brought us from Hong Kong to Canton a few months before.

By 1940, Japan held Manchuria, North China, down to the Yellow River and the Yangtse up to the gorges (between Ichang and Chunking) and, as we have seen, seven of China's most important cities and all the major ports. She set up blockades to prevent the movement of goods. She blocked the Burma Road, the main source of supply for the wartime Nationalist capital at Chungking. She encircled Hong Kong, not only cutting it off from the rest of China but also burning and looting all the villages on the Chinese side of the border. This led to an increasing influx of refugees into Hong Kong. Foreign wives and children were evacuated from the smaller treaty ports and businessmen retreated as their work became impossible. All over China, refugees were on the move.

Japan carefully watched the progress of the war in Europe. She saw Nazi Germany conquering all before her. The German armies seemed unstoppable. In the West she saw France fall before the jackboot in June 1940 and the setting up of the puppet Vichy government in that country. England looked vulnerable and would probably be the next to collapse. Germany would surely conquer Europe; why then should Japan not do the same in the Far East and divide the world between them? In August, Japan put pressure on Vichy France to grant her air bases in Northern Indo–China. In September this was followed by the signing of a tripartite pact with Germany and Italy. This bound Japan to enter the European war on the side of Germany and Italy if America should enter it on behalf of Britain. In April 1941 Japan signed a non-aggression pact with Russia and, in July, established a joint protectorate of the whole of Indo–China with Vichy France. This last act caused America to sever her trading relations with Japan. Britain and the Netherlands followed suit, which meant that the Japanese could no longer import oil from the Dutch East Indies. These oil supplies were vital if Japan were to continue her military campaigns. As she had every intention of doing so it was evident that Japan would soon be joining the Axis powers in the World War against Britain and her allies. When the warlike General Tojo took charge of Japan in October 1941 there was no turning back.

In Canton, we had been used to curfew on the river starting at 7 p.m. every evening and lasting until 7 a.m., an inconvenience but something we could live with. However, as 1941 progressed, the Japanese in occupation became more and more truculent and provocative towards the foreigners. They were very pleased with themselves and riding high – their armies hadn't experienced defeat and they were sure they were invincible. Adjacent to our house on the riverfront was a Japanese military establishment. I would watch the soldiers disporting themselves in their G-strings, doing bayonet practice and generally showing how clever they were in the martial arts. In October, the Japanese set up a pontoon in front of the landing stage for Shameen and searched everybody who disembarked. Indignant protests from foreign consulates were made, to no avail. The Japanese, at this stage, were in a mood to do whatever they wanted. In view of the grave international situation at this time, the British Consul advised that all British women and children should leave China as soon as possible. The exodus began. Ma, in the hope that we wouldn't have to go, rather dragged her feet. Had she no children, she would have dismissed any thought of leaving. I remember her pacing up and down the veranda in a state of agonised indecision. Pop made the decision for her. 'You'll have to go,' he said. 'I can't bear to think what might happen if you are caught.'

Japan Enters the Second World War

Once again our family was to be broken up, and on this occasion for a much longer period than previously. Ma, Moira and I waved Pop goodbye. It was a sad parting as we left for Hong Kong on the 3 December on the SS *Fatshan*. This British ship had been berthed on the other side of the river opposite to our wharf for the ten months we had lived in Canton. That same evening we arrived in Hong Kong and were met by a Jardine's representative and were taken to the Harbour View Hotel, Kowloon. Our passage from China had been booked on the SS *Tanda*, which was due into Hong Kong from North China at the end of December, bound for Australia. However, our plans to travel to Australia by that ship were overtaken by events. On the 5 December we were told to be ready to leave the following day as the last refugee ship with British nationals on board had arrived in Hong Kong harbour. This was our last chance to escape. Before we left, we were lucky enough to meet our old friend Bill O'Neil again. On one evening we were entertained by him in his flat and then on the following evening he invited us to have a Chinese meal with him at the Hong Kong Hotel. On the afternoon of the 6 December the three of us with our eleven trunks went out across the harbour in a motor boat and boarded the

SS *Anhui*. It was a scruffy-looking ship painted a dismal grey. It was crawling with humanity, all of whom seemed to be looking over the side, watching our forlorn family coming aboard. The ship was designed for seventy passengers but there were some 300 packed like sardines into the vessel. We were shown to our quarters – a space cleared away on the ground in the bowels of the ship below the waterline. Ma refused to accept it and said we would be the first to drown if the ship were hit. We were taken to the next level and shown some bunks. The accommodation was better but the stench of unwashed humanity forced us to vacate those quarters and settle ourselves on deck.

We huddled together for warmth. Before reaching Hong Kong, the *Anhui* had collected British nationals at Tientsin and Shanghai as it sailed down the coast of China. At Hong Kong we were the last to embark on that overcrowded ship. There was a large number of Indians on board, bound for their homeland. The white British were to tranship at Singapore for Australia. As we sat rather dejectedly on deck, quite unexpectedly we received an invitation to have dinner at Captain Evans' table. This was our last civilised meal for some considerable time. As night fell we weighed anchor and set sail for Singapore.

On the morning of the 8 December, the captain announced that the American naval base at Pearl Harbor in Honolulu, Hawaii, had been attacked by Japanese planes. In consequence Great Britain and

America were now at war with Japan. We were advised that, due to the danger of travelling on the high seas, the captain had been instructed to change course and make for the nearest friendly port. We were now heading for Manila, the capital of the Philippine Islands, situated on Luzon, the largest island of the group. These islands were ceded to the United States of America after the Spanish–American war of 1898. We were all issued with life belts and told to keep them with us at all times. Also, there would be blackout regulations in force. On 9 December we arrived in Manila Bay. We weren't alone, it seemed that all the merchant ships in the vicinity had made for the same shelter. The bay was full of vessels awaiting the next move. We learnt, to our surprise, that among the ships in the harbour was the SS *Tanda*, the vessel on which we had booked to take us from Hong Kong to Australia at the end of the month. At 12.30 p.m. on the 10 December, the war reached us. We heard the drone of planes. I rushed to the ship's railings to look up. There in the sky I could see a mass of tiny silvery planes in V formation, with the sun shining on their wings, looking like a swarm of firefly. The main target was the American naval base at Cavite in Manila Bay. Bombs rained down, destroying naval shipping and shore installations. The planes then directed their attention to the ships in the harbour. The SS *Anchung*, the nearest ship to us, about eighty feet away, was hit twice. Some pieces of shrapnel struck our decks but, thank goodness, no one was hurt. Other ships in the harbour were also damaged. Lifeboats were to be seen desperately rowing ashore. Ninety per cent of our passengers were women and children, most of whom sought shelter below deck. We opted to stay on deck as the safest place should an evacuation of the ship be necessary. To keep up their spirits, those who went below sang songs and hymns. As I heard the strains of 'Nearer my God to Thee' wafting up from below, I thought how strangely reminiscent it was of the sinking of the *Titanic* to the accompaniment of music. Not a very comforting thought. After the raid was over, wise old soldiers among us said the Japanese would be back that night to finish off their work amid the glow of burning hulks and the blazing coastline to light their way. They were proved wrong, thank God.

The next morning, the 11 December, we were told that the captain would not continue his journey with us on board as he was not expected to take responsibility for our safety in the present conditions. We must all leave the ship. One missionary family refused to go. We disembarked with our hand luggage, which amounted to one suitcase each. All our heavy items had to remain on board. We heard later that Captain Evans had decided to make a dash for it and the *Anhui* had slipped out of Manila harbour that very night and had made it safely to Australia. The bulk of the passengers were taken to the Manila Club. We were sorted into groups and our party of sixty were taken to the Caloocan Golf Club in the northern outskirts of Manila. The club itself had been deserted so we had it all to ourselves. The club house was pleasantly situated on the edge of a very attractive golf course. It seemed as if we had received the best accommodation going of all the groups that had been billeted around Manila. We made ourselves as comfortable as we could in this artificial situation. We knew it was only a matter of time before the Japanese would arrive – it was an eerie sensation.

The assault on the Philippines was launched from the island of Formosa (Taiwan), some 400 miles to the north of Luzon. Apart from the bombing raid we had experienced in Manila Bay, the top priority was to strike the American airfields. At Clark Field on Luzon, all the B17 flying fortress bombers were destroyed on the ground. Nichols and Nielson Fields near Manila were rendered inoperative. A three-pronged ground attack on Luzon was planned. General Homma landed to the north of Manila at Lingayen on Christmas Eve; General Morioka brought his troops ashore at Lamon Bay to the south east of Manila and a third force landed at Legaspi in south eastern Luzon.

While all this activity was going on, we in Caloocan Golf Club could do nothing but wait upon events. At Christmas we had a tree which the children decorated and a few presents were exchanged. It all seemed a bit strange, celebrating peace on earth with a determined enemy closing in on us on all sides. On New Year's Eve we realised it was only a matter of days, if not hours before the arrival of the Japanese army. Some-one sensibly suggested that we should dispose of all the alcoholic liquid on the premises. Practically all the men and women in the group and the larger children like Moira and me helped in the operation. We started at 6 p.m. and finished at about eleven o'clock. Bottles were broken and their contents poured down the drain. Some of the helpers couldn't bear to see this happen and buried many of the bottles in the ground around the clubhouse. Moira and I assisted in the burying operation. There were still a few who helped themselves liberally to the precious liquid before reluctantly disposing of it. When all traces of alcoholic drinks had gone, we relaxed with some food washed down with soft drinks. At midnight we all joined hands and sang 'Auld Lang Syne'. It was a touching moment. Many of the women broke down. We all retired to bed – 1941 was behind us.

In the New Year, General Douglas MacArthur, commander of the US Forces in the Far East, declared Manila an open city. This meant it would not be defended. US troops retreated to the Bataan Peninsular and, on 2 January 1942, the Japanese forces entered the city. At the golf club it was thought prudent to keep our young women out of sight to minimise any risk to them and Moira, at thirteen years old, joined the others in their hidden quarters. On the morning of the 4 January, a six-foot tall Japanese colonel with impeccable English arrived at the club. To introduce himself he told us he was an Oxford graduate and his father was interned in London. He went on to say that his troops had occupied the city and would soon visit us. We were not to worry, we would be well looked after. We must, however, put a white flag on the gate to alert them of our presence.

The next morning several trucks arrived with a small contingent of Japanese soldiers shouting and gesticulating. We collected our few belongings and some food supplies and were told to line up outside the clubhouse to be counted. This was a long tedious operation. When our captors were satisfied, the women and children were separated from the men who, after touching farewells from their womenfolk, were driven off. We were then bundled into the remaining trucks. We travelled south, crossing the Pasig River which cuts Manila in half from east to west and were set down at Villamor Hall, one of the halls of residence of the University of the Philippines. Unknown to us, this was where the first civilian prisoners were processed before being taken to a place of more permanent detention. When we got there, who should we see but the men in our party who had set off from the golf club ahead of us. After being counted to ensure we were still all present, our whole group of sixty people was allocated two music rooms, measuring 8' by 20', on the second floor of the building. It seems all the British nationals were put on this floor. The rooms were empty. We just made ourselves as comfortable as we could on the floor. An adjoining room was full of British merchant seamen from the SS *Tantalus*, a ship that had been in the harbour with us on the 10 December. They were all sitting on the floor looking listless and dejected. These men had been rounded up by the Japanese on the 2 January and dumped in the room without any food or water until we arrived on the 5 January. We immediately shared our food supplies with them.

For the remainder of that day and through the night we were closely guarded. Next morning, we were taken outside, counted and recounted. The men were then driven away and we followed as before. After a short journey going north and re-crossing the Pasig River, we turned into Calle Espana and stopped at the main entrance to the University of Santo Tomas, founded by the Spanish in 1611. It was known affectionately as the oldest university under the American flag. This was to be our home for over three years and known to us as Santo Tomas Internment Camp.

Internment – 1942

The university had an extensive campus surrounding a number of buildings. In the centre of the complex was the main building, by far the largest on the site. It was four storeys high and was to accommodate both men, women and children from ten years of age and over. To the right was the education building, which was earmarked for men and older teenage boys. Behind the main building was the annexe designed for women and for their children under the age of ten years. To the right of the annexe was a structure which served as the camp's first general hospital, manned by our own interned doctors and nurses. Adjacent to the main building on the left was the seminary, which housed the Dominican order of priests who ran the university in normal times. They were cordoned off from the camp by a high barbed-wire fence. Immediately in front of the priests' territory at the edge of the campus was the gymnasium where the elderly men were to be placed. This camp accommodation was to house between 3,500 and 4,000 internees during their enforced stay under the Japanese occupation of Manila. A small restaurant, used by the students of the university in peaceful times, between the main and education buildings became the commandant's office. By the main gate were the quarters of the Japanese Guard.

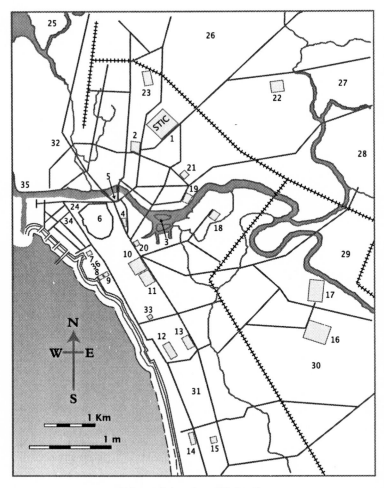

Plan of the city of Manila
from James E McCall: Santo Tomas Internment Camp

City of Manila Legend

1 University of Santo Tomas. Santo Tomas Internment Camp.
2 Bilibid Viejo.

3   Hospicio de San Jose.
4   City Hall.
5   Post Office.
6   Walled City (Intramuros).
7   Manila Hotel.
8   Army and Navy Club.
9   Elks Club.
10   University of the Philippines.
11   Philippines General Hospital.
12   Rizal Stadium.
13   De la Salle College.
14   Manila Polo Club.
15   Park Avenue School (Military prisoners interned here and employed on Nielson air field).
16   South Cemetery.
17   Santa Ana Race Tracks.
18   Manila Gas Plant.
19   Malacanan Palace.
20   Legislative Building.
21   Holy Ghost College.
22   Quezon Institute (Santol Sanatorium).
23   San Lazaro Race Tracks.
24   Fort Santiago.
25   Balut Island.
26   Santa Mesa.
27   New Manila.
28   San Juan.
29   Mandaluyong.
30   Makati.
31   Pasay.
32   Tondo.
33   Remedios Hospital.
34   Port Area and Piers.
35   Mouth of Pasig River.
36   Luneta.

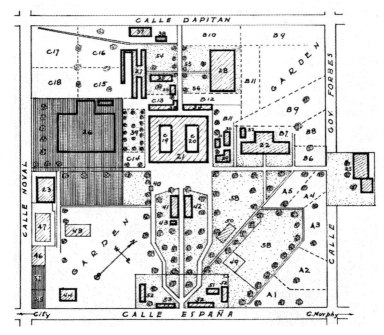

Plan of Santo Tomas Internment Camp
from James E McCall: Santo Tomas Internment Camp

Legend

(Shaded portions represent the restricted area, about 11 acres)

1   20 inclusive, Shanty areas.
21   Main Building.
22   Education Building.
23   Gymnasium Building.
24   Package Shed Office.
25   Santa Catalina Hospital.
26   Dominican Seminary and Church.
27   Diet Kitchen and Children's Dormitory.

28 Isolation Hospital.
29 Commandant's Office.
30 Carpenter Shop.
31 Soft Diet Kitchen.
32 Tiendas.
33 Camp Outside Kitchen.
34 Dining Sheds.
35 Model Home Children's Playhouse.
36 Finance and Supply Bodegas.
37 Japanese Food Bodega.
38 Japanese Guard House.
39 Padre's Garden.
40 Dave Harvey's Stage.
41 Classrooms.
42 Plumbing Shop and Sanitation Bodega.
43 Shoe and Cot Repairing.
44 Duck Farm.
45 Printing Office (closed).
46 Camp Baggage Bodega.
47 Reserve Water Supply (swimming pool).
48 Concrete Court.
49 Indoor Baseball Diamond.
50 Basket Ball Court.
51 Package Shed.
52 Japanese Guard Quarters.
53 Japanese Guard House (office).
54 Children's Playground.
55 Incinerator.
56 Public Clothes Lines.
57 Vacant Lot (restricted area).
58 Open Lawns (used for storage of Jap supplies).

The 6 January 1942, the day we arrived, was the date on which the largest number of civilian prisoners of war had been brought to Santo Tomas by the Japanese. The scene was chaotic. Each group had to be counted and agreed. The counting and recounting went on for some time, with shouting by the Japanese and forlorn and worried prisoners standing around on the large concourse in front of the main building hoping something would be sorted out. Some thirty of the women and children from the Caloocan Golf Club, including ourselves, were eventually directed up to Room forty-eight, a bare room with a cold stone floor, on the third floor of the main building. For two weeks we used our coats to sleep on, then mattresses were supplied together with mosquito nets. We slept in this fashion, on the floor, huddled together for some six months until beds were provided by the Red Cross: unadorned wooden structures upon which the mattresses we had received earlier could be placed. Ma and Moira got one of these beds each. I acquired a camp bed, which I used throughout my internment.

The initiative for organising the camp had to come from the internees themselves as the Japanese showed little interest in directing operations. However, they insisted on the institution of roll-call after breakfast in the morning and again at nine o'clock in the evening. An executive committee of leading figures was set up and an American, Earl Carroll, was elected first chairman. Sub-committees were spawned to deal with every aspect of camp life: camp order, work assignment, safety, sanitation, education, religion, recreation and many more. Any approaches to the commandant would have to be made through the executive committee. Interpreters were also appointed to break down the language barrier between the Japanese and those internees who needed to communicate with them. One such appointee was a British man, Mr Stanley. Over the following years most internees thought him to be a collaborator, as he seemed to be working very closely on a day-to-day basis with the commandant and his staff. He remained a mystery throughout our internment.

Most people accepted the inevitable and tried to come to terms with their new lifestyle. Some could not and a number of escapes were attempted in the first few weeks. All escapees were recaptured. On the 11 February, three young Britons, Thomas Fletcher (twenty-nine years), Blakey Leacock (twenty-five years) and Henry Weeks (twenty-eight years) went over the wall with the intention of trying to get to the American troops on Bataan, but like the others, they too were soon recaptured. The Japanese authorities decided to make an example of these escapees. They were brought back to camp and brutally beaten. The monitors of their rooms were called to the commandant's office and taken out of camp to watch the execution of these young men. Each was stood in front of his shallow grave and shot. As they fell into their graves, their bodies were immediately buried without ceremony. There were no more attempted escapes.

Stanley
from James E McCall: Santo Tomas Internment Camp

In broad terms, seventy per cent of the camp population were Americans, twenty-eight per cent were British and the last two per cent accounted for a sprinkling of Dutch, Polish, Russian, Mexican and a few others. The predominant ethos in camp was American. As early as January 1942 a school for the many children in captivity was started. It was based on American lines.

Mrs Lois F Croft, the principal of the American School in Manila and Pasco E Lautzenhiser, the principal of H A Bordner School, also in Manila formed the camp school which was up and running by the 22 January. It provided the basic subjects of English, Arithmetic, Science and History. It was held on the top floor of the main building, where the science laboratories of the university used to function. It was a grade school. I began in grade six. Moira in the grade above. School was in the morning. Some homework was given each day, all of which could be despatched pretty expeditiously some time in the afternoon and the rest of the day was our own. I never felt I accomplished very much at the school. We learnt a lot of American history and by the end I felt I was an expert on the Red Indian tribes but little else. When history was being taught in Moira's class and it touched on the British Empire, if some snide remark was made by an American student about 'the Limeys', Moira would rush to the defence of Britain. Most of her classmates were Americans and she felt obliged to be the spokesperson for Britain. On the other hand, if she was with a group of British youngsters and a nasty comment was made against America, she would stand up for the Stars and Stripes.

With the commencement of school, both Moira and I began to make friends. I was always interested in what was going on in the big wide world and an older boy, possibly two years older than I, seemed to be the ideal companion. Roy Fernandez appeared to have a fund of knowledge on every conceivable subject under the sun. He had come from Shanghai and was with us on the SS *Anhui* which brought us to Manila. On the subject of sex he was most helpful. Moira and I were as innocent as Adam and Eve before the fall. Within a few weeks in camp our eyes were opened; it was as though we too had eaten the forbidden fruit. Roy, whom I respected greatly, put me right on this delicate matter but I needed some convincing. My first reaction was to say 'I don't believe you. My parents just wouldn't do that sort of thing.'

'If they didn't,' he replied bluntly, 'you wouldn't be here today.' That ended the first discussion on this subject. He told me about the Battle of Britain and the few who had defeated the mighty Luftwaffe over England's skies. He described the skill and bravery of the Spitfire pilots. All these events had occurred less than eighteen months before. It was as good and exciting to me as any documentary on the war. Roy explained the concept of Commonwealth to me and all sorts of subjects that hadn't ever crossed my mind. He told me that after the war he would go to Australia and take up politics. In the event, I discovered many years later that he had gone into the diplomatic service in Australia and had become a senior diplomat. He was a good friend and I thoroughly enjoyed his company.

The central kitchen, sited on the ground floor at the back of the main building opened on 31 January 1942. It catered for some 3,000 internees each day with only four serving counters, which meant about 750 hungry people for each outlet. The women and children in the annexe and the internees in the camp hospital were catered for in their own part of the camp. Breakfast was cracked wheat, a sort of porridge. We called it 'mush'. There were dead weevils in this gruel – these foreign bodies had escaped the eagle eyes of our labour force of weevil-picking women, of whom Ma was one. The gruel was washed down with a tin mug of tea. Lunch was watery rice fortified by a few vegetables, which might have included camotes (sweet potatoes), talinum (sort of spinach) or some cabbage. Our evening meal was slightly more substantial – a rice base plus a modest portion of gravy with vegetables and some grisly meat plus the usual mug of tea. The dining sheds were behind the main building. Roughly-hewn long tables and benches adequately served their purpose. In the early days the meals, though of poor quality, were sufficient to sustain us through the day. To supplement the ration, those who had lived in Manila had servants or friends who were allowed to deliver parcels of food at the front gate each day. Six hundred parcels were received on an average day and it was said some 800 to 1,000 in the camp benefited from these deliveries. This facility was allowed until February 1944 when a sterner regime took over the camp and any privileges were stopped. At this early stage in our camp life some thought was given to those who had not been residents of Manila and had nobody outside to bring them goodies to the gate. An adoption system was devised. Well-meaning citizens of Manila who wanted to help could adopt somebody in camp and from time to time deliver a gift of food or some other comfort for their adoptee. Mrs Lobrigat, a Spanish lady who owned a music shop nominated my mother as her choice as they seemed to have a common bond in their interest in music. On the occasions we received a parcel from Mrs Lobrigat it was a great treat for us to be able to enhance our drab meals with the contents of her package. In addition there were some enterprising entrepreneurs in the camp who were able to cook small items of food which could be purchased by internees if they had the money. However, there was still a large number of those in the camp who had to rely on the basic food ration to survive.

In the seminary, there lived Spanish Dominican priests who were not interned, as Spain had not entered the war. Among them were two American priests, Fr McMahon and Fr Ahern, who for the time being were allowed to stay with their community and also come into camp to say Mass for us. They gave some fine sermons, living up to their name as members of the order of preachers. In addition, an Irish priest, Fr Patrick Kelly of the Columban Order, whose parish was in the Malate district of Manila, came into the camp on Sundays. He too was not interned as he was from the Irish Free State, and Southern Ireland was not in the war.

The Columban Order had been founded in Ireland in 1916 as a missionary society for China. The first priests of the society arrived in that country in 1920. By 1928, the need for such priests was urgently required in the Philippines and Archbishop Michael O'Doherty of Manila pleaded for the Columban Fathers to come and start missionary work in his diocese. In May 1929 the first two Columbans arrived in Manila to take up their work at Malate church, Fathers Michael Cuddigan and Patrick Kelly. Others followed shortly afterwards. Fr Kelly became the first Columban parish priest in the Philippines. He was known and loved by all. He visited the homes and walked the streets of the parish and was a familiar figure to everyone. When the Second World War reached the Philippines after Pearl Harbor in December 1941, Fr Kelly was allowed by the Japanese to visit Santo Tomas Internment Camp where he said Mass every Sunday from early 1942 to the middle of 1943. His Mass was said on the fourth floor of the main building on the laboratory tables where the camp school functioned during the week. I offered to serve his Mass as I had been well trained as an altar boy in Shanghai – my mother had taught me the Latin prayers when I was eight years old. On his Sunday visits, Fr Kelly was a focal point for personal messages. Not only did he bring information from outside from friends but he also took back to his parish in Manila details of camp life and passed on news to his parishioners from their friends in Santo Tomas. It is surprising to me that the Japanese allowed him to come into camp for so long a period. It was not until June 1943 that he was banned from further entry into camp. During his visits I regularly served his Mass. I used to kneel on the cold stone floor for months, when suddenly Fr Kelly gave me a small bean bag, explaining that a young girl attending the Mass had felt sorry for me kneeling on the hard floor and had made it for me to use at Mass. It is with regret that I never discovered who this kind little girl was and so was not able to thank her personally. As soon as Fr Kelly was told he could no longer continue his Sunday visits to the camp, he gave me a prayer book as a small thank you present. He inscribed it, 'In remembrance of your faithful service at Holy Mass, to Desmond Malone, Santo Tomas IC, Manila. God bless you always'. It was dated 3 June 1943. I was touched by his gift and have treasured it ever since. Fr Kelly was a devout elderly priest who worked in his parish all through the harsh years of the occupation. That is, until Manila fell to the returning US forces early in 1945.

One feature of camp life was the shanty. As early as the beginning of February 1942, the first were being built. More followed and a shantytown community emerged. The construction materials could be obtained through the package line if one had the money to purchase these items and the necessary arrangements could be made for their delivery. This shanty building was a form of escapism, to get away from the hurly burly of day-to-day camp life. There were twenty designated areas where such edifices could be erected, mainly around the periphery of the camp grounds. Ma and I, with Mrs Bowen and her son Gerald decided to build a shanty for ourselves. As we were early on the scene there was plenty of land and Gerald and I staked out a large plot on the eastern corner of the camp. We didn't have the expertise to build a properly constructed shanty, nor the means to obtain the materials. After some scrounging we ended up with a shack with sawali (Filipino matting) for the sides and roof and some planks on the ground to give a wooden floor. We tried to compensate for our lack of construction skills by designing an attractive garden. We cultivated the ground outside the shack with grass and flowers and a pebble path up to the entrance. I had acquired a Filipino scythe, a small implement with a curved blade. The user would squat in the long grass, grab a tuft of grass in one hand and with the other use the scythe to cut the grass below where it was being held. The operator would work on the patch where he had started and then move on when that space was clear. It was a slow but effective way of getting rid of an overgrown area. I used the scythe in this way and was doing very well until my enthusiasm got the better

Dave Harvey
from James E McCall: Santo Tomas Internment Camp

Santo Tomas internment Camp, patio scene

produced by Double Delta Industries Inc. the National Archives and Records Administration, Maryland

of me and I cut too high under the grass tuft I was holding and cut a nasty slice in my little finger. That stopped the operation immediately. I still have a faint scar where it happened, to remind me of the incident. When all was ready, the two mothers arrived with deckchairs to enjoy the peace of their new surroundings. After a short time the Bowens stopped coming to our makeshift retreat. Perhaps it wasn't quite the idyllic spot they had hoped. Ma and I continued to use it quite regularly. Moira visited the shack occasionally but wasn't terribly impressed. One day an incident occurred with a couple of snakes, which can best be described by a little poem Ma and I made up in rhyming couplets after the incident.

The Snakes

A lady was sitting in her shack
When an uproar was heard behind her back
Her son cried out with panic and fear
'Don't move, don't move I pray, Mother dear.'
She looked alarmed, and he said 'Look there,
See, there's a snake crawling under your chair.'
The neighbours came from round about
With sticks and with brooms, the snake to clout
The snake tried to hide inside a jar
But a man pulled him out with a thin iron bar.
Another man came and the onlookers thrilled
For with one mighty blow, the snake he killed.

The neighbours dispersed each one to his home
With fervent hopes no more snakes would roam
But to each and everyone's dismay,
A little later in the day,
A second one came to find his mate
Only to suffer a similar fate.
Now mother and son can sit in their shack
And know that those snakes will never come back.

As the building of very professional-looking shanties started to happen all around us, there was strong pressure on us to give up our piece of land to one of the big boys. We could see we were being squeezed out and, after some persuasion, Ma accepted $100 HK from the Coote family – Mr and Mrs Coote and their two teenage sons Blow and Kenny. Mr Coote was the manager of a Texan wrestler, Danny Dousek, a colourful character who was also in the camp. They built a magnificent shanty on stilts with wooden stairs leading up to the entrance. Our prime site served them well and they used every inch of our land to build their splendid edifice – the land we had so generously staked out for ourselves.

It was not long before the entertainments committee arranged 'floor shows' for us. It was a very important morale booster. The leading light in this occupation was Dave Harvey, a nightclub entertainer before internment.

There were two patios in the main building. A patio in this instance is a form of garden courtyard overlooked by the building on four sides. The east patio was designated an area for internees to erect shacks for their own use. The west patio was used by Dave Harvey to put on shows most Saturday nights. Sing-songs were organised there on Wednesday evenings. The commandant and his staff had an area of prime viewing set aside for them. Should they wish to attend on a particular evening, nothing of course could start until they arrived. On their appearance the band would strike up 'Hail, hail, the gangs all here, what the hell do we care, what the hell do we care, hail, hail the gangs all here, what the hell do we care now.' Wreathed in smiles, the Japanese contingent took their places determined to enter into the spirit of the occasion.

In due time the patio was seen to be too cramped for performances and the entertainments committee sought and received permission from the commandant to use the plaza in front of the main building for their shows. A large well-built wooden stage was erected with its back to the enclosed seminary compound. The new area was dubbed the Theatre under the Stars. However, the concourse was too busy an open space for chairs and other obstructions to be placed there permanently. Nevertheless, on the day of the show, chairs could be put down in the plaza from 5.30 p.m. Keen internees, hungry for entertainment, would surround the area with their seats. At a given signal there would be a mad rush to the centre and an almighty scrum followed, in a frantic bid to find the best viewing spots for the show. Like all the others, I too was waiting there. With my competitive spirit and my determination to succeed, I was nominated by Ma and Moira as the obvious choice for this task. By 5.35 p.m. the auditorium was full of seats with the exception of one carefully marked-out area. This was reserved for our guests, the commandant and his staff.

Allied to the start of entertainment was the setting up of a broadcasting system with the primary object of giving out camp news and orders and directives from the commandant's office. It proved an effective 'radio station' and a focal point for information. It was also a source of entertainment. In the Fathers' Garden, which was a grassy area adjacent to the Spanish priests' seminary building, a recorded programme of classical music was provided on certain afternoons. Ma tried to get there whenever possible to have an hour or so relaxing in the soothing atmosphere. From 7.45–8.45 p.m. on the plaza in front of the main building, lighter and more popular music was played. This entertainment ended just before curfew at 9 p.m. I often joined Ma and her friends sitting in their deck-chairs, chin-wagging until the strains of the signature tune, 'Goodnight Sweetheart', was played, signalling the end of the day. This last song was accompanied by the clack-clack of the closing deckchairs as the weary internees made their way indoors.

While we were busily settling ourselves into a routine of camp life, the war was going apace and the Japanese forces seemed to be having it all their own way. They naturally wanted us all to know about their success and to share in their glory so the English-language, Japanese-controlled *Tribune* circulated freely in the camp. The first big jolt we received was to hear of the fall of Singapore on the 15 February 1942. It was a bitter blow to the British to read of the surrender by Lieutenant General Percival to the Japanese commander-in-chief. We Brits had to suffer a lot of gibes from the Americans about our impregnable fortress of the East when their forces were still holding out at Bataan and Corregidor, not too many miles from us in Manila. Their turn was soon to come. General MacArthur left the Philippines in March to take command of the war from Australia, succeeding General Wavell as Chief of Allied forces in the Pacific. On the 9 April, Bataan fell to the Japanese, who captured 36,000 allied prisoners. They had been holding out on half rations for about three months and, by the closing stages of their defence of the peninsula, they were down to 700 calories a day. As they surrendered, more than 15,000 of the allied soldiers were clubbed down, shot or bayoneted to death. The remainder were forced to march sixty-five miles in the baking sun on meagre rations to their prison camps in Cabanatuan, north of Manila and to Bilibid prison in Manila itself, a stone's throw away from Santo Tomas. The horror of their death march was told by the few who survived. America's last hold on the Philippines ended with the fall of Corregidor on the 6 May, with the surrender of 10,000 US and Filipino troops by General Wainwright to the Japanese command. The only consolation now for the POWs and the civilian internees alike was General MacArthur's promise as he left for Australia 'I shall return.'

On the 2 July, following the fall of Bataan and Corregidor we received some seventy Army and Navy nurses who arrived in three truckloads from that embattled area where the American heroic last stand in the Philippines took place. It was a great bonus for our camp to receive this additional medical help for our own hospital staff.

On 17 June, a group of wives and children of British diplomats were repatriated. Thirty-three of them left for Lourenco Marques in Mozambique on the east coast of Africa where they were to tranship for England. Among the party was Mrs Prismall, a lady living in Ma and Moira's room. She took messages for Ma's family in England. She travelled with her son Robin. Since the early camp days Robin and I were great friends and on his departure I missed his company very much. Mr Prismall was left behind.

While on the subject of the movement of internees in and out of camp, Ma had the opportunity of returning with Moira and me to Shanghai. She went through the motions of completing the appropriate application form but heard nothing more. How the selection was made we shall never know. I would have thought our family had a prime claim to return to Shanghai, with five members of our family, including Pop, in two camps in the Shanghai area. However, on the 12 September, 113 internees left by ship for China.

From the stories which filtered back of their travelling conditions, packed in like sardines with horses and mules as travelling companions, it was perhaps a good thing we weren't selected for the journey.

The natural elements gave some unwelcome colour to our lives in camp in 1942; something which could not be blamed on the Japanese. On the night of the 9 April we experienced violent crashes and eruptions and the whole building shook alarmingly. On the campus, trees were uprooted and a number of shanties collapsed. We were experiencing an earthquake, something not uncommon in that part of the world. Being in our quake-proof building, we were lucky but those outside our camp in smaller and less well-built dwellings must have suffered badly. Following this experience, two months later the rainy season began. We were not prepared for its first onslaught. June had been very hot, with temperatures over 100°Fahrenheit, when suddenly the rains arrived on the fifteenth. Within twenty-four hours, seventeen inches had fallen and the whole of the camp grounds were awash. All of us remained indoors, apart from a few of the shanty dwellers who ventured out to rescue some of their belongings from the water and mud that abounded. The enforced overcrowding within the buildings in the hot steamy atmosphere was a most unpleasant experience. What a relief it was when the waters subsided and we could get out in the fresh air again.

Turning now to a few domestic details in the camp. On the 27 July, Earl Carroll, the chairman of the internees executive committee, which administered the camp for the Japanese, resigned his post and was replaced by Carrol C Grinnell. This was the senior camp committee and was answerable to the commandant for its actions.

Mr Grinnell remained a conscientious chairman of the committee until the end of internment. In his prominent position he was, in addition, deemed to be responsible for and to concur with any actions taken by his subcommittees, including any communications to the Japanese authorities, expressing anxiety, complaints or criticisms at the way internees were being treated.

One glimmer of light occurred on 24 August when we saw the opening of our permanent camp hospital – Santa Catalina – premises attached to the north-eastern side of the compound, approached through a gate from the camp. The ground floor housed a chapel and the kitchen area, with stairs leading to two large rooms, one for the women patients and the other for the men. This was a great improvement on the hospital facilities we had up to that time. The original hospital near the children's annexe behind the main building became the isolation hospital.

In October, our captors sought to make our camp more secure and to isolate it from the outside world. Ten feet within the camp's perimeter wall, barbed wire was erected. This would enable the Japanese guards to patrol the outskirts of the grounds unhindered. In addition, sawali, Filipino matting was put up to cover the railings above the wall to stop prying eyes from looking into the camp and to prevent us from looking out.

Of all the events that occurred in 1942, the one that affected me more than any other was my transfer in November, at the age of twelve, from room forty-eight – a room that accommodated women and children, where I lived with Ma and Moira – to room sixty, a room solely for men. The new accommodation was on the same floor in the main building as room forty-eight and it housed some fifty internees, men of all ages and every description. I set up my camp bed in the space provided for me. It was overhung by a large wooden bed used by Mr De Haan, a pleasant quiet Dutchman in his fifties. He kept a fatherly eye on me and advised me when he felt it was necessary to do so. One particular task which called for periodical attention was to deal with the bed bugs. These blood sucking little creatures clustered in the corners of the mosquito net and also in the nooks and crannies of my camp bed. Every so often I washed my mosquito net at the washing troughs in the back of the camp and then took it along to Mr Henry Ford, an American bank manager in normal times, who had a large cauldron of strongly disinfected water where the nets were dunked. His was a flourishing activity always, with long queues for his decontaminating operation. After drying the net in the hot sun, not a bed bug survived. As for my camp bed, after a thorough scrub and winkling out of the little creatures from their hiding places in the wood, the hot sun did the rest. After the operation, a smiling Mr De Haan with a pat on my head reassured me that I had done a good job. Captain Bulteel, the room monitor, was a British seafarer who had captained merchant ships in the China seas. A short but well-built man, he was about five feet tall with a large commanding voice more suitable for a man twice his size. He left no one in doubt as to who was in charge. I was pleased to be in his room, feeling independent and learning to fend for myself – I had become a man!

Shortly before Christmas 1942, rumours were circulating that the Americans were to receive food parcels from the American Red Cross; comfort kits, as they were popularly called. The reason it was thought to be for the Americans was that the number of parcels to be received coincided with the number of US citizens in the camp. Some of our more vociferous US inmates were cock-a-hoop about the generosity of Uncle Sam, who always looked after his own. 'You Limeys will have to sit and watch us feasting ourselves,' they said, 'and wonder when your lot will think about sending you something.' On the 17 December, the parcels arrived. In the event, they had not come from Uncle Sam but had been sent from South Africa from the British Red Cross in that country. What is more, there was a parcel for everyone in the camp. On their arrival, all the ill feeling that was experienced before they came evaporated. The parcels were a little larger than a shoe box but were gratefully accepted. These were the first comfort kits we had received and we all strove to eke out the contents for as long as possible.

As 1942 came to a close, our theme song 'Everything's Gonna be Lousy' composed by Dave Harvey, our camp entertainer, caught the mood of the internees in the early days of their camp life. Here is a sample of the ditty:

Our lot is getting better and the country getting wetter,
So I'm no longer sad and pessimistic,
Conditions are chaotic, but I'm very patriotic,
And I want to show that I am optimistic.
I wouldn't say a word to make you blue – oh no,
I've come to bring a word of joy to you,
Cheer up, everything's gonna be lousy.

You eat your mush without any milk in the morning,
But the prune juice works in the same old-fashioned
    way,
You may have been the president of Manila's leading
    store,
But you've still gotta haul the garbage from the third
    and highest floor,
You may grumble now at the beans and peas,
But wait till you start on the bark of the trees,
Cheer up, everything's gonna be lousy.

I've plenty to be thankful for although it's hard to bear,
things could be a darn sight worse, although I don't
    know where,
Don't think that I'm complaining 'cause it really's not
    the case,

And if I look disgusted, why, it's just my natural face,
I haven't a pot to cook in, but at least I have a bed,
It may belong to the Red Cross, but it's a place to lay
  my head,
So smile and show your dimples, they're worth their
  weight in gold,
You may as well my friends, before you know it you'll
  be old,
Cheer up, everything's gonna be lousy.

The lines are getting longer just like the ones on your
  face,
But wait, till you're five years older and you're still in
  the same old place,
The rumours may be all that you need,
But you'll soon begin to believe what you read,
Cheer up, everything's gonna be lousy.

Internment – 1943

Early in 1943 I began to be aware that I had some aptitude in the field of sport. Football was my first love. I knew it was a team game but, as I thought my skills were better than most of the others, I tended to hog the ball and considered individual skills to be paramount – I had a lot to learn. We were forced to call our game 'soccer' as the Americans called their game 'football'. In American football, the ball, which is like a small rugger ball, seldom touches the foot, so where the name of their game came from remains a mystery to me. Adult soccer teams were formed into a league and exciting matches took place on Sundays and Thursdays at 6 p.m. I used to run the line. One of the teams was the 'Tantalus' named after the British merchant ship they sailed in. This was the group of men we had met when we were rounded up by the Japanese on 5 January 1942 and dumped in Villamor Hall. Our enthusiastic little football group befriended one of the team. He was known as Lumps. Not only did he acquire a splendid football for us, which I undertook to look after, but he also gave us football tuition. He was one of the older members of his team and played fullback. Lumps gave us a good insight into how the game ought to be played. There were enough of us to make up two teams. We reluctantly accepted a few American boys to add to the numbers. I called my team 'the Spurs' and Stanley Baker, a young lad about my own age took over the other team, which he called 'the Saints'. We had regular matches against each other. They generally took place after 3 p.m. on certain days, in the heat of the sun. I remember one particular match when the temperature was 103° Fahrenheit in the shade. It was a desperate game which we won, but we were all pouring with perspiration and exhausted. I fell upon the water fountain and must have drunk it dry. I thought I was going to die of heart failure. Luckily we had the sense not to repeat this experience when the sun was really hot. Lumps continued to train the more enthusiastic of us and we used to ask him how we compared in skill with the boys in England our own age. He eventually gave us his considered opinion – we were as good as any youngsters England had produced. We all went off feeling very pleased with ourselves, believing implicitly everything Lumps had said.

I was introduced to Basketball and was as good as the rest in general play but I never reached any distinction in shooting. However, we had a great time in the basketball league, playing on several afternoons in the week. I was very proud that during my captaincy, our team became league champions. We were awarded a bamboo cup with handle with the names of the team painted on its side. At the same time, they had a vote among the players to choose one of us who had shown the greatest sportsmanship throughout the competition. To my delight I won that award and was given another bamboo cup with a suitable inscription on it. These trophies remained a memento of those days for many years afterwards. An adult basketball league was formed and the skill of these players was amazing. I was always impressed with the Pan-Am team, who seemed to be larger and more skilful than any opposition.

The big attraction in the adult evening games was the softball league, played four times a week starting at 6 p.m. This game is, in essence, baseball with a soft ball – suitable for playing within our camp grounds without any fear of the ball being hit over the wall. The Giants, the Dodgers, the Pirates, the Braves and others were slogging it out and making home runs, to the delight of the excited supporters.

In many ways I enjoyed the first two years of captivity in spite of the poor quality of the food. I liked the degree of independence camp life gave me. After morning school and some homework, which could be finished by early afternoon, the rest of the day was my own. Moira was doing her own thing with her teenage friends and Ma was attending to her camp duties and afterwards either listening to music in the Fathers' Garden or socialising with her friends. A feature of camp life was the siesta hour every afternoon from 1– 3 p.m. This rest was needed because of the intense heat at that time of the day. I usually spent the two hours following the siesta out of doors until the evening meal, which started at 5 p.m.

After the meal and the sporting activities that followed, as mentioned earlier, I sometimes joined Ma at about 7.30 p.m. in the sitting-out area in front of the main building where music provided the backdrop for a social get-together before the curfew at 9 p.m. when we were all required to be indoors for the night. Outside our room we had to line up in the corridor for roll-call, which usually lasted about ten minutes. Occasionally, we were advised that the commandant and members of his staff would be inspecting us and this entailed a long and tedious wait of say thirty to forty minutes. When the Japanese party arrived with the camp interpreter, at a given signal we all bowed from the waist in unison. The commandant satisfied himself that all were present and his party then walked up and down the serried ranks as though it was a military parade and then departed for their next port of call. Not until the commandant had returned to his office could the camp, as a whole, be dismissed.

It was my habit after roll-call to go round to my old room to see Ma before I got ready for bed. I whistled my special signal to alert her I was outside. We would have a short chat with a few scraps to eat, if Ma had managed to acquire anything, before I departed for the night. Incidentally, during the course of 1943, at the age of fifteen, Moira decided to leave room forty-eight to go and live with a number of her friends on the ground floor. This move enabled her to get away from a room full of older women and also to be free from any parental control. We saw her from time to time but she really preferred to live with and have the company of a younger set of people.

After taking leave of my mother and returning to my room, being a creature of habit, I made for the washroom at exactly 9.30 p.m. each night. The adjoining room was occupied by a number of American Catholic priests of the Order of Oblates of Mary Immaculate, who had been brought into our camp late in 1942 from Cotabato, a town on the island of Mindanao. Some of these priests would sit outside the room in the corridor reading their breviaries. One of them commented that I was so regular passing their room every night that they could set their watch by me.

In the washroom we were fortunate to have plenty of water. There was no hot water but we soon learned that a good refreshing cold shower did wonders. The lavatory facilities were not so congenial. When I had an urgent need to use them, the most alarming sight was to find a long queue of desperate, half naked, sweating men all waiting for the same thing. Five cubicles, from which the doors had been removed for other purposes, were less than adequate for the hundreds of men entitled to use those facilities. When my turn eventually came, it was no comfort to have those anxious heavy-breathing figures hanging over me, watching my every move, when I was trying to have a quiet moment to myself. At less popular times of the day I could be more composed as I sat there. I would look at the graffiti on the walls. Apart from the expected crude drawings, there were rhymes and other comments. Two I remember: 'Here I sit, broken-hearted, paid a penny and never farted.' The other was an admonition; 'If you can't do it, get out and let somebody else in who can'.

In addition to the priests from Cotabato, there were many more from all over the Philippines, taken from their mission fields and brought into our camp by the end of 1942. Eventually, there were fifty-four priests living within the walls of Santo Tomas prison camp. As I was a well-trained altar boy I offered my services to these priests. Each morning, starting at 6 a.m. the Masses began. They used to take place in the laboratories on the fourth floor of the main building, where the school functioned later on in the morning and where I served Fr Kelly's Mass on Sundays when he was still allowed to come into the camp. It was convenient for me to get there as it took place on the floor above my room. I was able to serve three Masses, which took me up to 7.15 a.m. when it was time for me to join the long breakfast queue for my weevil-peppered mush and tin mug of tea. My religious activities were not confined to the morning Masses. I was drawn into the Devotions at Santa Catalina chapel where the Rosary and Benediction took place every Sunday evening. In May and October, Our Lady's months, there was the Rosary, the Litany of Our Lady and Benediction every evening. Likewise in June, the month of the Sacred Heart of Jesus, we had the Litany of the Sacred Heart followed by Benediction every day. I seemed to be the only young lad in the whole camp who was prepared to give up his time and use his skills as an altar boy. In spite of denying myself the pleasures of the evening sporting activities in the camp in the months of May, June and October, I would probably have been most disappointed if another young boy had appeared to help me out. I wouldn't have felt so indispensable as when doing all these activities on my own and it was this which spurred me on and enabled me not to miss the occasions when I was needed.

During those days, Ma was able to use and develop her abilities as a singer. She joined the camp choir, run at that time by Mr Backerini-Booth, and she sang soprano solos with other leading members of the choir, including Mrs Backerini-Booth who had a fine contralto voice. This interest in music and singing gave Ma great pleasure and pushed her worries into the background. We had received no news of my father since we left him behind in Canton in December 1941.

One fascinating aspect of life in Santo Tomas was the variety of characters who roamed the camp. Mr Casera was the rat-catcher from the sanitation department – you were secure from vermin when he was around. Sid was the Australian ex-boxer who had spent more years in the ring than were good for him. Most evenings he was present outside the central kitchen area at about 6 p.m. when the serving hatches had been closed. Scuffles broke out for the few watery scraps that had been slopped on the counter when the food was being given out and Sid was always in the thick of it. His lack of coordination often found him spreadeagled on the ground. I always felt a pang of sorrow for him as I made my way past this desperate scene.

There was a strange lady we called Pocahontas – in her early forties with heavily hooded eyes, her dark hair plaited in one thick braid which extended well below her waist. She wore a faded flowery patterned dress held in by a long black woollen belt.

Another sight was a man in his sixties who had vowed neither to dress nor cut his hair while he was imprisoned in the camp. He wandered about with well-worn silk pyjamas and carpet slippers. His grey hair was long and greasy, covering his shoulders and curling at the edges. Under his arm was his chipped enamel plate always ready for the next meal.

Yet another character was the self-assured 'Captain', a man in his late forties with a contented expression, tweaking his well-waxed upturned moustache, sporting a handsomely trimmed beard. He wore a dark open necked shirt above a pair of well-worn breeches. His shins were encased in leather supports which rested on stout army boots and under his arm was a horsehair broom to keep the flies off. He clutched a wooden tray and held a tin bowl with eating utensils and a small enamel mug for his tea. He was ready at a moment's notice to join any queue offering food.

There was also seen from time to time a curious little rotund man wearing a sombrero. His preoccupation was to pull behind him an open-backed wicker chair as he walked to provide him with much needed rest as the day proceeded. Another character was the Texan wrestler, Danny Dousek. When he first came into camp at the beginning of 1942 he was a mountain of flesh – a frightening hulk of humanity to the eyes of an eleven-year-old boy. After losing seven stone in weight he looked a very large man but with a well-defined figure. He appeared from time to time in a Texan outfit with a ten-gallon hat and high-stepping boots, a very impressive sight. These characters and many others helped to colour the fabric of camp life.

Early in 1943 Santo Tomas was getting very crowded. In addition, there were 2,000 enemy nationals out on passes in Manila, some in hospitals in the city, such as the Philippines General Hospital and Hospicio de San Jose. A large number on conditional releases and a few hundred Catholic and Protestant clergy on temporary release. All these and other special cases were liable to be called back to camp by the Japanese military authorities. The solution to this problem of overcrowding was to start an overflow camp. On the 9 May, the commandant announced that a site had been found for a new camp at Los Banos, about a hundred kilometres south of Manila on the shores of a great inland lake, the Laguna de Bay. It was presented as an idyllic spot, a veritable health resort. 800 young men were to be ready in five days to travel to Los Banos to build barracks on the site for themselves and for more internees to follow when the new camp was ready. Volunteers were called for – the response was lukewarm. 275 bachelors signed on. The rest would have to be press-ganged. A list was prepared from unattached men and young married men. Many of those chosen tried to get out of it with a variety of excuses. None but those with the most compelling reasons were allowed to have their names withdrawn. On the appointed day, the 800 who had been mustered departed in army trucks for their new assignment.

On the 31 August 1943 there was a census of Santo Tomas internment camp. This census was to include those residing outside the camp in hospitals and institutions in Manila and all the others living in the city on permanent and temporary passes. For those actually living in the camp, the statistics revealed that there were 3,848 internees in total, 2,803 Americans, 939 British (including Canadians and Australians), fifty-four Dutch and the remaining fifty-two consisted of Norwegians, Spanish, Polish, French (De Gaullists), Egyptians and Swiss nationals. Outside the camp there were an additional 3,026, which included the 800 young men sent to Los Banos in May. The rest were in Manila with valid reasons for being out of the camp.

While on the subject of statistics, I should mention that the facility of the package line at the front gate began as early as January 1942 and continued until it was closed by the Japanese military authorities in February 1944. It enabled 800–1,000 internees to receive packages each day from outside the camp. The contents were mainly foodstuffs but other items could be received provided they didn't look suspicious. In this way, those with money and good contacts outside, in addition to those who had generous friends in Manila, could work out a relatively comfortable life for themselves and handsomely supplement their food ration with those extra items. *Tiendas* (stalls) at which goodies could be bought began to spring up in the camp. I remember one stall where an enterprising operator used to cook a form of pancake which looked very appetising. Dare I say it, they sold like hot cakes!

We, as a family, didn't avail ourselves of much of this extra cuisine and had to rely on the food line for our sustenance. Gradually, two classes of inmates emerged, the Haves and the Have-nots. We were firmly in the latter category. I decided, in 1943, I should get a job so that perhaps we too could buy a few of the items from the camp *tiendas*. The sort of paid occupation available to me as a thirteen-year-old boy was a fetching and carrying job. Mr McCort and Mr Schnider, two elderly American gentlemen who had a shanty in a distant corner of shanty town, which was approached through long grass, gave me the job I was looking for. In the early evening, before the food line was open, I collected their meal tickets and tins and made my way to the central kitchen to be early in the queue to get their meals. When I returned to their shack I was required to fill up all their receptacles with water from a nearby standpipe to leave them with a sufficient amount until I returned the next evening. After performing one or two other minor jobs, I was dismissed with an imperious wave of the hand. These two men always seemed to be locked in earnest conversation putting the world to rights and hardly noticed my presence while I was ministering to their needs. Mr Schnider, the dismissive hand-waver, was the taller of the two. He had aquiline features and held himself well with military bearing. He had an authoritative air about him. I assessed him as a first generation American whose parents had emigrated from the Fatherland. He would not have looked out of place as a commander in Hitler's army. His companion, Mr McCort, was a less impressive figure. He was short, with a chubby round rosy face with small stubby features but with a well-groomed grey beard. He had a high-pitched voice. He looked like an ageing gnome. I was paid every Friday evening in 'Mickey Mouse' money. This was the name we gave to the highly inflated Japanese currency, which replaced the Filipino peso during the occupation. Unfortunately, I was forced to give up the job after only a few months. The lack of nutritious food was starting to take its toll. Four journeys to and from the central kitchen through the long grass was exhausting me. When finished, I then had to queue up for my own food with my cracked enamelled plate and mug before the line closed. I cannot think that the paltry sum I was paid, which I passed over to Ma, added very much to improve our situation in the camp.

In August 1943, a general code of regulations for the camp was promulgated by the camp's executive committee with the approval of the commandant. It was drawn up for the information and government of all the internees. It superseded any previous rules and regulations. It was a very exacting document and covered every aspect of camp life. It extended to seventy-five articles and told us exactly what we were to do and not to do. It gave us a code of practice which was to govern our activities for the rest of our camp days. It appeared that the commandant was happy for the internee officials of the camp, provided he was kept informed, to administer the rules and regulations and settle any problems or disputes and even impose punishment if appropriate. Only if matters were serious would the commandant have to step in and deal personally with the problem. Many of the rules were irksome and irritating but those on sanitation, hygiene and safety were well thought out and beneficial. We were fortunate to have well-organised committees who effectively ran the camp and formed a buffer between ourselves and the commandant and his staff.

In July, without a formal announcement, there was a strong rumour that a repatriation list was being drawn up. It seems it was for those in the camp who had a history of illness. Provided a medical certificate was issued by one of the camp doctors, such a person would be considered. Ma, who in other circumstances would have jumped at the opportunity to return to England, did not wish to try. Pop was presumably still in China with the rest of his family and we expected to return to China after the war and continue living in that country. In any event, it seemed to be for sickly people and we as a family had been reasonably healthy. There was obviously substance in that rumour. On the 31 August, a notice was posted on the camp bulletin board announcing that a repatriation ship would sail at the end of September. It would be made up of Americans, Canadians, British and a few Dutch. However, on the 20 September a further notice appeared on the board. The bald heading to the statement, 'British repatriation cancelled', said it all in a nutshell. It was a bitter blow for those British internees who had hoped to go. Early on the morning of 26 September 1943, a happy party of 119 repatriates left the camp for their homeland.

The rainy season in 1943 arrived as in previous years. July was wetter than usual, with thirty-six inches of rain in that month when something in the region of nineteen inches was the norm. However, this was small beer compared with what was to follow. In the middle of November we were hit by a typhoon. Torrential rain and heavy winds lasted for a couple of days. Rain penetrated everywhere causing flooding, and the winds gave our shanty town a severe beating, with many shanties collapsed from the storm. There was misery everywhere while it lasted. The typhoon hit Los Banos as well and destroyed much of the work our men had completed since their arrival from Santo Tomas in May. Their activities had already been hampered by the summer rains but the typhoon had greatly added to their problems. A large number of women were anxious to leave Santo Tomas to be reunited with their men folk in Los Banos and many other internees wanted to go in the hope of a better life for themselves in the new surroundings. Finally, on the 10 December 1943, the first group of Santo Tomas inmates left for the new camp.

As 1943 was coming to a close, the entertainments committee decided to put on a pantomime for Christmas and the New Year. Cinderella was the choice. Many of the camp teenagers volunteered to take part. Moira was among them and was chosen as Prince Charming and one of her close friends, Wendy Gates, was Cinderella. They all worked hard at rehearsals and when the show came on in the Theatre under the Stars, as we called the large concourse in front of the main building, it was a great success. It was performed on Dave Harvey's large, well-constructed stage, sited at the south-western end of the open area with its back to the seminary grounds.

Fr McMullen, one of the English missionary priests whom we all knew, remarked to Ma how well he thought Moira had acted and how refreshing it was to hear a clear, nicely-spoken English voice on the stage.

By the end of 1943 we had received three Red Cross parcels since coming into camp. In December 1942, the comfort kits from South Africa arrived. Hard on their heels in January 1943 the Canadian Red Cross sent a larger package for each of us, full of tins of food, powdered milk and other luxuries. Finally, in December 1943, our last Red Cross relief supplies came from the American Red Cross; an even larger package for us all. We were advised to eke out the contents gradually to supplement our camp diet, which was getting increasingly meagre as time went on. Some managed rather better than others. Moira chose the fast track and finished her Red Cross supplies far quicker than most of us. Good luck to her.

And so to the end of 1943 with two full years of camp life under our belt – what would the next year bring? There was a saying in those days that Spain had held the Philippines for 400 years, America for forty and the Japanese would hold it for four years. It seemed that this prediction might well come true.

Internment – 1944

On a teenager's sixteenth birthday he was regarded as having come of age and was required to enlist for camp duties. In January 1944, many of Moira's friends had obtained jobs in the central kitchen. She didn't want to be left out, so anticipating her sixteenth birthday by six months she joined the kitchen staff. The men did the strenuous work of carrying the heavy cauldrons of prepared food to their required position and the girls were given the job of serving out the food to the internees. The central kitchen, as we have seen earlier, catered for some 3,000 internees with four outlets, 750 people for each line. Moira had bitten off quite a job for herself. She was issued with a white hospital apron with CK printed on the front in indelible ink. She was also required to wear a bandana to keep her hair out of the food. She, like all the others, had to undergo a physical examination to ensure she was fit for the job. This was repeated from time to time throughout the year. All the camp inmates were issued with a meal ticket, which lasted a calendar month, and before the meal the ticket was punched for the appropriate meal of that day. Moira had arrived at her job in the kitchen at a most sensitive time. Food was getting so short that inspectors were posted behind the girls to ensure that they didn't give out a bit more of the carefully

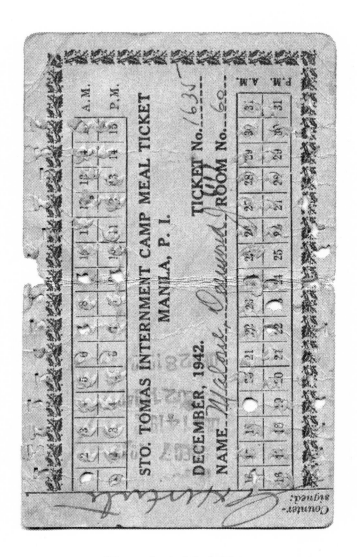

The author's Meal ticket,
December, 1942

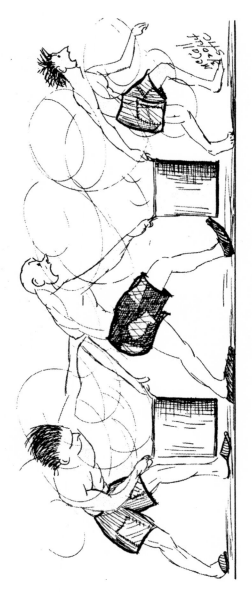

'Gangway! Hot stew!'

from James E McCall: Santo Tomas Internment Camp

The dining sheds

from James E McCall: Santo Tomas Internment Camp

measured portions to their friends and families. If a person was caught doing this it would mean a fine and instant dismissal from the kitchen. In November of that year, Moira was found giving extra to her friend Vera Bulling and was dismissed from the kitchen and fined. All was forgiven by December and she was reinstated. She was, however, watched like a hawk there afterwards but she didn't have a second lapse.

On the question of food, the dawn of 1944 heralded an important change in the administration of this vital commodity. Food requirements up to that time had been appropriated on a day to day basis according to our needs from our supplies held in *bodegas* (warehouses) in the camp. The daily allocation was, of course, subject to an overall limit and availability. On the 24 January a letter from our civilian commandant Mr K Kato advised us that with effect from the 1 February, the Japanese military authorities would in future furnish supplies of food to the camp. These would be allocated on a per capita daily basis amounting to 766 grams a day for persons eleven years of age and over. Children under eleven years would get half the ration. The items to be supplied would be fish, cereal, vegetables, sugar, salt, cooking fat and tea. Over the course of the year, due to erratic deliveries, these stocks of food dwindled to a dangerous level. It was not long before fish, sugar and cooking oil disappeared from our diet. To exacerbate the food problem, the package line was brought to an end in February.

Apart from food, another cause for concern in those

early months of 1944 was the treatment of certain prisoners in the camp by the Japanese military authorities. Three signatories who were described as agents of the internees of Manila internment camp wrote a letter of complaint in April via our camp commandant to the representative of the protecting power of the United States in Tokyo, under the Geneva Convention of 1929. The complaint concerned five internees who were alleged to have brought into camp certain typewritten transcripts containing war news. One of their number, J H Blair, was taken to the guardhouse on the morning of 25 February, severely beaten about the head and over his kidneys with a rubber hose and tied up for the rest of the day. He was returned to his quarters at 5.30 p.m. He had a terrible night in great pain, passing quantities of blood in his urine. On 1 April he was called from his hospital bed to report to the commanding officer. He was made to walk to the guardhouse and was never seen or heard of again. The other four were taken out of camp at the end of February and they also disappeared.

There were several other instances of beatings and maltreatment complained of to the commandant by the representatives of the internees. The only response from the Japanese was that the senior agent, Mr C A Dewitt, was banished to Los Banos camp in October and the internee agents' committee ceased to function.

As 1944 progressed, batches of Santo Tomas internees were being transferred to Los Banos. Those who wanted to go had convinced themselves that they were going to a better place. When they arrived at this new abode they found it was not quite as welcoming as they had been led to believe. Stretched endlessly across the campus were long wooden barracks, each divided into fifty cubicles, six feet by eight feet, separated from each other by flimsy *sawali* matting. These partitions were just five feet high and did not allow much privacy. Outside the cubicles was a five foot wide passage which ran the length of the barracks. The *nipa* roof, made from palm tree branches, which was hardly more sturdy than the *sawali* matting, was clearly no guarantee that the barrack's dweller would have a roof over his head in angry weather conditions. It was, however, enjoyed as a home by a variety of bugs. Each cubicle was totally bare and the new occupants had to make their empty quarters as liveable-in as best they could with the possessions they had brought and with the help of willing workers in the camp. The new arrivals were soon to discover that the use of water was to be a problem. It is true there were a few drinking water taps about the camp and some running water was available for showers and the washing troughs, but water to flush the lavatories was primitive in the extreme. Each barracks had a small lavatory cistern. This container was to provide the flushing facility for a hundred men, women and children. Nearby there was a standpipe. From there twenty buckets of water were needed to flush out the system. They were tipped into the shoulder-high receptacle and the water persuaded to work its way through all the lavatories of the barracks. If this backbreaking exercise went well, the waste material would be piped away beyond the camp. If blockages occurred, the stench became intolerable but could be dealt with quickly within the camp's boundaries. If the blockage took place after the sewage had left the camp, out of bounds for internees, they would have to wait until the Japanese sorted out the problem. This could take days. Having left Santo Tomas with its substantial buildings, plenty of running water for all occasions and food no worse than they were now receiving, undoubtedly many Los Banos inmates would rue the day they made the decision to volunteer for the new camp.

Back in Santo Tomas, Ma's camp duties up to about the middle of 1944 had been to work with the weevil-picking brigade of women who extracted those nasty little insects out of our daily cereal before it was cooked. In August 1944 she was transferred to do the same task at Santa Catalina, the camp's main hospital, at the extreme north-east side of the camp. This was a great improvement as the best of the food was sent to the hospital and it was a small group of women who did this work in more comfortable surroundings. She had her meals on the hospital premises. It was fortunate that the move came when it did, as Ma had been very run down from camp life and had come out in a series of carbuncles under her arms – these are like large boils with eight or nine heads. It was most debilitating for her. Although her condition went on for months and she was suffering considerably, she was very stoical about it and I never heard her complain.

As mentioned earlier in this account, by the end of

1942 most of the Catholic missionary priests who had been working throughout the Philippines had been rounded up and brought to our camp. Among them were four English priests, Frs Deegan, McMullen, Timmons and McCann, who were members of St Joseph's Missionary Society at Mill Hill in London. By the middle of 1944, Fr Timmons joined me for dinner every evening. It may be that since my father was not in the camp he might have felt that his presence as a father figure might be helpful for me. We got our meal, such as it was, from the main kitchen, and would go up to the third floor and sit in the corridor outside Ma's room where we had a table and chairs. Beside us sat Mrs Zennor. She shared Ma's room with some thirty other women. All her meals were eaten outside the room, sitting at her large round metal table. She was a tall woman, perhaps in her early fifties. She carried herself well, with a touch of elegance about her posture. Her hair was carefully combed back off her face to reveal an unsmiling countenance. It seems that she was absorbed in her own thoughts and didn't need to communicate with others. She hardly uttered a word to us all the time we were sitting next to her during our evening meals. Eating was her abiding passion. When her spoon had scraped off all it could from her tin plate, she would raise the plate to her lips and lick off what was left with her tongue. This activity was conducted in a very genteel fashion. Nevertheless Fr Timmons was taken aback when he saw this operation for the first time. He whispered to me that he was quite shocked and surprised that this woman should lower her standards in this way. It was my turn to be surprised that, in all the circumstances, Mrs Zennor's breach of etiquette should provoke any comment at all. Although a bit stuffy on that occasion, Fr Timmons was a jovial man, a good raconteur, and I enjoyed his company at dinner very much.

As a newly ordained priest, Fr Timmons was appointed to the Philippines and arrived in the town of Iloilo on the island of Panay in November 1931. He served as a curate in a few of the parishes in the locality of the town and by 1935 became a parish priest. In July 1939 he was sent to Manila to be one of the private secretaries of Archbishop Michael O'Doherty and in March 1940 returned to Iloilo to continue his life as a parish priest. In August 1942, along with other priests in the region, he was rounded up by the Japanese authorities and interned with us in Santo Tomas Internment camp. When he first arrived in camp at thirty-nine years of age, he was a rotund prelate of benevolent disposition who gave me the impression that he would never pass up an invitation to a hearty meal. He slimmed down considerably as time went on, but never lost his pleasant demeanour. During our meals, Fr Timmons would entertain me with stories of his life in his Philippine parishes and how different it was from working as a priest in England.

Here is a sample of amusing incidents that had kept him on his toes:

There was the occasion on a Sunday when Fr

Timmons was saying Mass. At the most solemn part, the Consecration, music was being played on the organ in dulcet tones – not an uncommon practice. However, the solemnity of the moment was instantly lost when he recognised the music as being the pop tune which was all the rage in England when he left; 'Ain't she sweet, walking down the street...'

Fr Timmons described how, as a zealous young priest, he had decided to improve the facilities of the church. He bought some fine pews for the women of the parish to use and put them in front of the altar. The churchgoers didn't know what to make of them. They had not seen anything like them before. It was unusual to have any form of seats in the churches of the more remote parishes. However, when the priest turned to face the congregation with the greeting 'Dominus Vobiscum' (The Lord be with you), he was unable to disguise his amusement when he saw all the women perched on top of the pews like a row of birds on a wall.

An activity which took some getting used to was the need his enthusiastic parishioners had for making a big show at Mass by having flying angels winging their way around the church during the service. These large dive-bombing plaster angels were a constant hazard to anybody in the way of their flight path. So far as I am aware, no serious accidents occurred but the practice had to stop.

In a more instructive vein, Fr Timmons explained that the way to convert the local inhabitants to

Christianity was to capitalise on those practices in the church which could be most closely related to their pagan form of worship. The Catholic use of statues was an obvious starting point. Fr Timmons thought that all would be well once he made the distinction between the Christian approach, where a statue was only there as a reminder of the heavenly personage, as opposed to the pagan practice of adoring the plaster icon itself, representing one of their gods. But more was obviously needed to drive the lesson home. One evening, going into the yard at the back of the presbytery he found the sacristan cleaning the statues from the church and selling the water to a long queue of women as holy water. The sacristan was astonished when his little sideline was stopped. Apart from thinking he was doing nothing wrong, he seemed to regard this activity as a legitimate perk of the job.

In the autumn of 1944, as well as amusing me with some of his stories to while away the evening meal with his young charge, Fr Timmons thought he might start teaching me a little Latin. This was a mistake, I was not responsive to his efforts. He told my mother that he thought I was too undernourished to concentrate on a new learning experience. It was disappointing that I was not able to learn Latin at this time as it would have helped me greatly in post camp days when I was at school in England.

Again, on the question of food, an internal report describing the Japanese Army's quantity of food issued to the camp's central kitchen during the period

February to June 1944 revealed that the ration amounted to 1490 calories per adult per day. It was pointed out that according to the Philippine Council of Nutrition, a man of eleven stone on light labour needed 3,000 calories a day. Such a man when lying quietly in bed needed 1850 calories and when asleep 1560 calories. The diet was disastrously low in protein with no eggs, cheese or milk. Vitamins and minerals were lacking as practically no fruit and only poor-quality vegetables were provided. The amount of calcium in the food was less than a quarter of that required by an adult.

So alarmed were the internees at the state of our food that on the 14 August 1944 the parents' committee sent a letter via the commandant of the camp addressed to the Commander in Chief of the Imperial Japanese Forces in the Philippines. The letter pointed out that during the previous six months the Japanese Army had reduced the official food ration from bare minimum to starvation level. By August there were no eggs, no milk, practically no fruit or other basic food-stuffs essential for children. The irony was that eggs, milk, bananas and peanuts could have been supplied to us as they were produced in large quantities in or near Manila.

By the latter part of September 1944, Japan had been at war with the Allies for nearly three years. The first two years of internment had been tolerable so far as food was concerned. The quality was below standard and nutrition value far from satisfactory but the quantity seemed adequate. From the start of 1944 when the Japanese military authorities took over the management of our food supplies, the situation went from bad to worse. We had been in Santo Tomas Internment camp since early January 1942 and our resistance was getting very low. However, there was light at the end of the tunnel.

On Thursday, 21 September 1944, our day as children started no differently from any other. At 9 a.m. we had, with great effort, reached our schoolroom on the top floor of the main building. I felt as weak as a kitten and not very interested in what was going to be taught that day. However, an event took place that morning which gave us all more stimulation and excitement than if a banquet had been set before us with no limit placed on what we could eat or drink.

The Japanese had held air manoeuvres overhead for some weeks and that Thursday seemed to be no exception. As we sat in our seats trying to concentrate on our school work, activity in the sky seemed more intense than usual. We then heard a distant drone which grew louder. By this time we were all distracted and looking out of the windows. To our amazement and excitement we saw wave after wave of American bombers high in the sky, glistening in the sun and, lower down, the fighter planes dive bombing. The whole building vibrated with the noise. It was only at this late stage that air raid sirens whined out across the city and a loudspeaker in the camp told us to take cover. We all tumbled down the stairs to our own quarters. This was it, we thought, the Americans are here. Everybody danced around in jubilation. The reality, of course, was that there would still be some months to wait before we were free.

When the euphoria died down there was anxiety amongst some of our older internees, who were seriously debilitated from almost three years of deprivation, which had left them in an advanced stage of malnutrition. With the continuing deterioration of the food situation, the question in their minds was who would be the first to arrive, the American liberating forces or the Grim Reaper?

At this stage it might be suitable to review the war in the Pacific. After the devastating attack on Pearl Harbor before dawn on Sunday 7 December 1941, destroying, in one blow, the US Pacific Fleet, the Japanese acted with speed. On 8 December, Wake and Guam islands fell. The naval base at Cavite in Manila Bay was completely destroyed by fire on 10 December. It was during this raid that Ma, Moira and I were on the SS *Anwhei* in Manila Bay, our refugee ship which had just arrived from Hong Kong. Also on the 10 December the Japanese made their first landing in the north of Luzon, the principal island of the Philippines. Disasters followed swiftly in Luzon – most of the American air forces were destroyed. On 21 December the main Japanese invasion force landed in Lingayen Gulf and marched on Manila, which they entered on 2 January 1942.

Elsewhere in the Pacific, the news was equally bad.

After stiff resistance, Hong Kong fell on Christmas Day. By the end of January 1942 the Japanese had landed on Borneo, New Guinea and on the Solomon Islands, just north-east of Australia. They advanced down the Malay peninsula and Singapore fell on 15 February.

On 8 March, Java capitulated to the Japanese. As General McArthur left the Philippines for Australia on 12 March he promised, 'I shall return'. He was made Chief of Allied Forces in the Pacific region, succeeding General Wavell, on 17 March 1942.

The Japanese took Bataan on the island of Luzon in the Philippines on 9 April, capturing 36,000 allied forces. In Burma, Mandalay fell on 2 May. The last American resistance in the Philippines collapsed on 6 May with the surrender of 10,000 US and Filipino troops on Corregidor, the fortress in Manila Bay. With this recital of Japanese whirlwind successes it was most heartening for the Allies to find a chink in their armour. This occurred when the invading forces were prevented from landing at Tulagi in the Solomon Islands and at Port Moresby in New Guinea. This first serious setback for the Japanese took place on 8 May 1942 – a straw in the wind which was to gather force and sweep the Japanese war machine, island by island, back to their homeland.

On 7 June the Japanese Navy was forced to withdraw after heavy sea and air fighting around Midway Island in which Admiral Chestor Nimitz claimed to have inflicted great damage on enemy ships. This action was regarded as the turning point in the Pacific War, six months to the day since Pearl Harbor had been attacked. On 23 September, Australian and US forces under General MacArthur began offensive action against the Japanese in New Guinea. By early February 1943, Japan had abandoned the Solomon Islands and withdrawn from New Guinea. By November the Gilbert Islands, north of the Solomons, had fallen into Allied hands and in January 1944 the Allies launched an assault on the Marshall Islands.

On 25 February 1944 the US Air Force attacked the Japanese bases on the Marianas and Guam, some 1,300 miles to the east of the Philippines. These islands were regarded by Japan as the bulwark guarding the way to the Philippines and Japan itself. By 27 July the island of Guam was taken by the Allies. It was from this base that, on 21 September, McArthur's air force launched an attack on the Japanese over Manila, the very air raid which we had witnessed in our classroom in Santo Tomas Internment Camp in the heart of Manila.

After that first Allied air raid, the commandant made the top floor of the main building out of bounds for all internees. This measure, we were told, was for our protection and safety. School was suspended and for practical purposes it was not resumed elsewhere in the camp. Apart from the listless pupils, the teachers themselves were feeling the strain of under-nourishment and malnutrition and, as time went on towards the end of the year, no lesser word than starvation was being used to describe our plight.

Apart from the essential services required to run the camp, there was little additional energy expended in any way. For the younger internees, all forms of sport had stopped and it had become a major effort to walk across the camp. I remember sitting at the bottom of the staircase of the main building, looking beyond the entrance doors that were always opened in the day to the grounds beyond. There, people were walking to and fro in what could have been a cinematograph sequence in slow motion. I then had a flight of fancy. I imagined that these moving figures would go slower and slower until they stopped and fossilised where they stood and remained there for ever more as a testimony to the inhuman neglect by the Japanese authorities of those in their charge during the Second World War.

On 7 October 1944, the parents' committee again wrote to the Commander in Chief of the Imperial Japanese Army in the Philippines as they had received no acknowledgement of their letter of 14 August. They reiterated the contents of their earlier letter and went on to explain that during the intervening weeks, the supply of food had been reduced to 300 grams per day for adults, which meant that children under ten-years-old received only 150 grams to keep them alive each day. The delivery of milk had been stopped and fruit and vegetables reduced to an insignificant amount. The Japanese authorities were providing the children of our camp with a small amount of cereal and practically nothing else. The parents complained vehemently about this seemingly deliberate policy of starvation. Nothing came of either letter and one is tempted to think they didn't even get further than the commandant's office.

There was some very heartening news in late October which raised the morale of the camp. There had been very persistent rumours that the US forces had landed in the Philippines on the island of Leyte. In a camp newscast over the loudspeaker system we were advised that there was a popular item in the camp shop which was selling like hotcakes. Those who had not yet tried to obtain this article should go straight away to the shop so as not to be disappointed. It was better to be '*leyte* than never'. This comment was picked up immediately and confirmed the rumour that the Americans had indeed landed on the island of Leyte. This reference to the landing of the US forces went over the heads of the Japanese and no repercussions followed. We learned later that General McArthur had said the Japanese navy had suffered its most crushing defeat in the Battle of Leyte Gulf on 20 October 1944.

By Christmas we had still not been freed. Our cereal supplies – rice and corn together with beans – had been reduced to 189 grams a day per head. To this was added a few vegetables, if and when available, and tea. On 20 December it was pleasing to hear from the internee committee that they had a small supply of jam and chocolate which they proposed to distribute to the internees for Christmas. A survey was carried out as to whether this little extra treat should be distributed through the central kitchen mixed up with our food to enhance our meagre rations, or given directly to each internee. The decision was overwhelmingly in favour of a direct issue to the internees. Each person then received the equivalent of one and a quarter table-spoons of jam and half a segment of chocolate on Christmas Day.

On the 31 December, Moira and her many young friends decided to see the New Year in. After 9 p.m. roll-call they all congregated on the third floor of the main building in the long corridors and had a sing-song to the strumming of guitars by some of the lads. At ten o'clock somebody produced a phonograph and they danced around till 11.45 p.m. at which time they all descended to the front lobby, making as much noise as possible. As the great clock at the top of the building struck twelve, they all sang 'Auld Lange Syne' with great gusto. The boys then chased the girls all over the place for half an hour. These youngsters then broke up into small groups to continue celebrating in their different ways. Moira and her very close friend Galina, together with my sister's latest boyfriend Charlie Schoenaube, went off to see the night through. By 3 a.m. Moira could not keep her eyes open and so went to bed. She and Galina dragged themselves out of bed for the 6 a.m. New Year's Day Mass before returning to sleep off their night's activities as they were not on duty that day.

Freedom at Last

January 1945 proved to be the most harrowing month for food, or rather the lack of it.

A not-unconnected event and one disturbing factor was the daily arrival, each morning, of roughly-hewn long wooden boxes to serve as coffins for the camp hospital. Later in the day a sombre cavalcade would trundle through the camp to the main gate with the bodies of those who had died within the last twenty-four hours. On one such occasion, the body of a tall man couldn't fit into the longest box and his legs stuck out about a foot beyond his coffin in a most undignified manner. It gave me a nasty turn as I saw it pass.

The news on the war front was getting better all the time. On the 9 January 1945, US troops landed at Lingayan Gulf on Luzon Island – 107 miles north of Manila. This news managed to filter through to the camp. It couldn't be long now before we were liberated – it was just as well. On that very same day, the commandant instructed the internee committee to announce to the camp that he was so sorry but he and his staff had discovered it was almost impossible to find any food in Manila. Accordingly, internees should make full use of facilities within the camp, making every effort to keep the gardens going at full capacity. A report at the end of January issued by our Internee

Food Procurement and Distribution Division confirmed this desperate situation. It stated that there was no doubt that January had been the most trying experience since the inception of the camp. The diet had been reduced to starvation level and it had been impossible to supplement the army ration.

My own physical state had deteriorated considerably. I suffered swollen ankles from severe malnutrition and on my fifteenth birthday, 27 January 1945, I was taken into the main camp hospital, Santa Catalina, weighing just four stone ten pounds. My mother told me later that the camp doctor had advised her that, given the same food conditions, I could last about another three months. She herself was taken into hospital in a similar condition a few days later. Moira seemed to fare better than we did. Her work in the kitchen serving out the food brought her in the category of special workers who got marginally extra food for heavy work in the camp.

The hospital was part of the camp although beyond its containing walls and I was introduced to the men's ward. It was a large room with windows overlooking the small garden below, where a young Japanese sentry marched up and down. I was allocated a bed in a row down the centre of the room – this had become available due to the death of one of the elderly internees. There was one young American lad about my age at the far end of the ward – he seemed to be the only other youngster in the room.

Fr McCann, one of the Mill Hill fathers, whom I knew well, was one of the orderlies in the hospital. He was a young vigorous man in his early thirties. Apart from his general duties in the ward, he seemed also to have the job of laying out the dead. This was a daily task and I came to take it all as part of the day's routine.

It was lights out in the ward at 9 p.m. and we lay quietly in our separate beds shrouded in mosquito nets. Most nights, not later than 9.30 p.m., Fr McCann would come to my bedside with some scrapings from the rice cauldrons in the kitchen discreetly wrapped, which he passed through to me under the mosquito net. He made a point of whispering, 'Eat it quietly and don't let anybody know or there will be a riot.' I would turn away from the nearest bed and put my head under the thin hospital blanket to munch the crackly morsels. I was very thankful that Fr McCann looked after me so well.

Saturday 3 February 1945 started like any other day in the hospital. The early morning routine went on as usual. Breakfast was the normal miniscule portion of tasteless watery mush served to each patient with a mug of tea. However, as the morning wore on we began to hear sporadic bursts of small arms fire and some air activity. This intensified as the day progressed. The battle for Manila was coming nearer. Unknown to us in the hospital, at about 10 a.m. ten American P38 fighter planes had flown over the main building, skimming the roof and dipping their wings. One pilot dropped his goggles with the following message tied to them, 'Your Christmas and New Year will be today or tomorrow'. There was great excitement and expectancy in the camp.

At about 6 p.m. somebody who was looking out of the window of our hospital ward to the compound below shouted, 'The sentry's gone – he's disappeared.' From outside the walls of the camp there were voices calling out to us, 'It won't be long now, Joe.' By this time we were all getting excited. We had heard of the recent landings of American forces in Lingayen Gulf in the northern half of Luzon and knew it was only a matter of time before we were freed. For weeks we had heard violent explosions where installations were being blown up in the city. Now we could hear the rumble of heavy armour – The Imperial Japanese Army was on the move, it seemed to be leaving town.

At about 9 p.m., hearing a commotion in the centre of the camp, those of us who could, strained through the window to see through the dark what was happening. Shouting, gunfire and flashing lights. The hospital was away from the centre of the camp, beyond the north-east retaining wall and all the action was taking place in front of the main buildings. Suddenly, a large American soldier burst into the ward. There was pandemonium – some rushed, others hobbled. We all went to meet the soldier to pat him on the back, shake his hand, embrace him. Fr McCann, who had been standing beside me, rushed over and hugged our visitor and danced around the room with him shouting, 'A real American soldier, a real American soldier,' like an excited little boy. He turned, picked me up and thrust me high in the air saying, 'You'll have sugar on your mush tomorrow morning.' That was like music

The Army takes over, 4 February 1945

from James E McCall: Santo Tomas Internment Camp

to my ears. That remark said it all – peace and plenty, the end of the war for us and the start of a new life free from hunger, hardship and imprisonment. The soldier was Carl Mydans, a former internee, a *Life* photographer who had been repatriated early in our camp days and had returned with the American troops. He was one of the first American soldiers to enter the camp. He soon discovered that his wife, Shelley, who had remained in the camp since his departure, was in Santa Catalina hospital and he had arrived to find her. What a reunion that must have been.

The next day I was discharged from the camp hospital. After all, there was nothing wrong with me that some good nourishing food couldn't cure. I sought my mother out in the women's ward and said goodbye to her. I left the hospital and walked along the path from Santa Catalina, in front of the education building on my right. Outwardly it seemed much the same as before. I soon learnt that on the previous night, five American tanks had crashed through the main gates of the camp while a hundred men scaled the matted spearheaded railings to storm and overpower the heavily guarded entrance. Meanwhile, Commandant Hayashi and some hundred of his men had entered the education building, holding 200 or so men and boys hostage. An attempt had been made to flush the Japanese out of the building. This had not yet been achieved.

On the left of my path as I walked back from the hospital was the main campus of the university. It was now an encampment for the US forces. Trucks, tanks, guns were everywhere; pitched tents, dug trenches and foxholes. These were surrounded by bazookas, howitzers and machine-guns. The troops were heating their rations over fires. All the impedimenta of the front line – a battle zone. In front of the main building, the atmosphere seemed relaxed. There were soldiers milling about and internees wandering here and there.

I went up to my room on the third floor, a room I shared with forty-six other male internees run by the redoubtable Captain Bulteel. My camp bed was there as before, still providing a home for bed bugs in the crevices of the wooden structure and in the corners of my mosquito net – nothing much seemed to have changed. The adjoining room was occupied as before by the Oblate Fathers – I had, after all, only been in the hospital a week, so why should anything have changed? I walked back along the stone corridor towards the stairs, glancing casually at our companion these last few years, carved from stone: the discus thrower poised, as ever, to discharge his missile. Down I went through the main entrance of the building. Wonderful smells assailed my nostrils – what caught my eye and excited me were the coffee stalls open for all to use and kiosks where items of food could be obtained. All of us in the camp were very conscious of our empty tummies and any chance of food or drink was like manna from heaven. I had a coffee, a bite to eat and immediately felt better.

The internees gathering there were talking of recent

events. One of them spoke of Carrol Grinnell, the chairman of the internees' executive committee. As head of the most senior committee in the camp he was responsible for the actions of all his sub-committees in their efforts to alleviate the hardships the internees were increasingly suffering. He paid heavily for his position. The Japanese removed him from the camp a day or so before we were liberated and he was never seen again.

I heard the story of the gallant Captain Manuel Colayco of Guerrilla Intelligence. At dusk on 3 February 1945, Captain Colayco was waiting in the northern outskirts of Manila for the arrival of the armoured brigade of the US 1st Cavalry Division. As the tanks appeared, Captain Colayco jumped into the jeep that headed the column of tanks, field guns, rocket launchers and one thousand men. He identified himself and with a carbine slung over his shoulder led the way to Santo Tomas internment camp. He was familiar with the city and all the hazards that would be encountered. He guided the column away from mined areas and tank traps, amid rifle and machine-gun fire, to the gates of the camp. As the US forces broke through the camp main gates, a Japanese grenade thrown from the garrison guarding the entrance exploded on the jeep in which Captain Colayco was riding. He emptied his gun on the enemy before he fell, mortally wounded. He died at a field hospital a few hours later.

There were other events which occurred on that

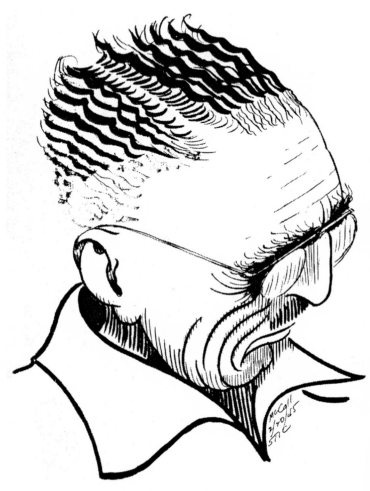

Carrol Grinnell
from James E McCall: Santo Tomas Internment Camp

*Lee Rogers and John C Todd, Santo Tomas survivors
from Prising, Robin,* Manila, Goodbye

evening – the most notable and revolting among them was the story of Lieutenant Abico, who was on the Japanese commandant's staff. He was thought to be responsible for the ever-decreasing ration of food we had received during the last few months until starvation level was reached in January 1945. This caused him to be hated more than any other Japanese in the camp. His story as I heard it was that when the US tanks arrived in front of the main building, Lieutenant Abico rushed out of his quarters, firing his revolver at the tanks. He was soon wounded and taken to the internees Red Cross clinic which functioned in a room just inside the main building. While being treated, but closely guarded, he attempted to blow up the room with a grenade he had about his person. He was quickly shot in the stomach and dragged out of the room to die. A crowd gathered around him like hunting dogs who had caught their quarry spitting, kicking, swearing at the dying man who was writhing on the floor drenched in blood, thrashing about in agony. The frenzied crowd stayed until they had worked off their venom on the poor wretch and then left him to die under the staircase. In my view, he was a Japanese soldier brought up in the highest traditions of the Japanese forces, with total dedication to his emperor and with unflinching loyalty.

The problem of the Japanese in the education building was soon to be resolved. Within twenty-four hours, an agreement was reached between the Americans, assisted by Mr Stanley, the camp's mystery man and British interpreter, and Commandant Hayashi, who had led the hundred-strong occupation party of Japanese the previous night. The enemy were to retain their weapons and be escorted en bloc to their front lines. Early in the morning of 5 February, headed by Commandant Hayashi, with Mr Stanley on one side and an American officer on the other, the Japanese contingent were marched out of the camp under heavy American guard. They were escorted to a point about half a mile from Santo Tomas. We heard no official version of what became of this forlorn group of Japanese, but rumours ran rife. The most favoured story was that an angry mob of Filipinos with hatchets and knives surrounded them and cut them to pieces.

It was learnt, about this time, that the much maligned Mr Stanley was, in fact, a British Intelligence officer, who throughout our camp days had been feeding information to the Allies.

While we were experiencing our first breath of freedom, other prisoners of war and civilian internees throughout Luzon were beginning to live through their version of that exciting event. On the 1 February, some twenty-five miles behind Japanese lines, seventy miles or so north of Manila, 120 members of the 26th US Rangers Battalion and nearly 300 Filipino guerrillas executed a daring commando raid on the POW camp at Cabanatuan. There they rescued 500 heroes of Bataan and Corregidor. Without delay, a rapid march was made back to base by many of the freed prisoners in spite of their enfeebled condition. Those who could not walk were carried by the Rangers or rode on carabao (water buffalo) carts.

On the night of the 3 February, when 3,785 of us were rescued by the 1st Cavalry Division, the 37th Infantry captured Bilibid prison, a stone's throw away from our camp, and released 800 POWs plus 550 civilian internees including women and children. The civilians included all those who had been interned at Baguio in Northern Luzon and had been brought down to Manila shortly before. Los Banos, our overflow camp of 2,146 internees fifty miles south of Manila, had to wait until nearly the end of February for their turn to be rescued. More of that later.

On the morning of the 7 February, in our camp, word went round that there was to be a ceremony of unfurling the Stars and Stripes. Crowds gathered in front of the main building and when all was ready with press photographers awaiting the event, Old Glory was solemnly hung from the balcony over the entrance. It was a touching moment and an attempt was made to sing 'God Bless America'. Some broke down, others waved and smiled, everyone was as happy as it was possible to be. That afternoon amid all the mayhem in Manila, General Douglas MacArthur, the Supreme Allied Commander, found time to make a brief visit to Santo Tomas. A vast number gathered in the foyer of the main building as soon as the news got around that he had come. It was a quick, spontaneous informal visit but a most exhilarating moment for us all.

One disturbing aspect of our life within Santo

Tomas at this early stage after liberation was that the Japanese in southern Manila were very much at large. They had entrenched themselves about a mile southwest of Santo Tomas in the walled city, Intramuros, in comparative safety, to fight back against the relentless American advance, which had crossed the Pasig river and was flushing out Japanese resistance wherever it was found.

From Intramuros, the Japanese trained their guns on our camp with the main building as their focal point, with its imposing tower which stood out as a very distinctive landmark. After a shaky start, when some of their shells fell short and others flew over the camp, by the evening of the 7 February, a devastating number of salvos hit their target. The southern corner of the building was badly damaged while other shells burst in the gymnasium, where our elderly male folk lived. The US forces didn't seem to have anticipated the attack on the camp and so no safety measure had been put in place. Before the evening was out, eleven ex internees were dead and more wounded. Two of Moira's young friends, who worked in the kitchen with her, were killed outright that evening. Annie Davis was only fifteen-years-old and Mildred Harper was nineteen. Up on the third floor, a shell hit the corner room of the main building and killed a kindly missionary, Dr Foley and blew off Mrs Foley's arm. It was the worst night we were to suffer in this way.

My mother, who had been in the camp hospital suffering from severe malnutrition, was discharged on the 8 February. She made her way back to the main camp as I had done a few days before. Reaching the top of the stone stairs on the third floor of the main building, she was confronted with a large pool of blood. Opposite this gruesome sight was a gaping hole in the corner of the building. This was the spot where Dr Foley had been killed the previous evening and his wife had been badly injured. It was clear that we were now in the front line with the strong US military presence in our midst who were firing back at the Japanese from our camp.

The 8 February gave us some respite from the shelling but still no safety precautions were announced by the US military to guard against future attacks. Perhaps they thought the first onslaught on us was a one-off and before the enemy had a chance to do any more damage to us they would be overwhelmed by US forces who were making rapid strides in the city. Another factor for this inaction might have been to avoid panic in the camp. After all, nearly 4,000 of us were still living cheek by jowl and the situation might have got out of hand. In the event, the shelling was not over, and we had to endure two more days of being shot at before the Japanese guns were silenced. In the late afternoon of the 9 February, Japanese shells again began to fall on the camp. Not until those enemy missiles were actually hitting our main building were orders for our safety given. Those of us, like myself, who lived in the front of the building, facing south-east, and those facing south-west, where my mother was situated, were most vulnerable to attack. People with rooms in those areas were instructed to go immediately to the back of the building and shelter behind it for safety. In fact, the whole of the southern side of the camp was vulnerable and we were warned not to go in that part until we were told it was safe to do so. Those of us who had a southern aspect were instructed not to go to our rooms for anything. I took this advice and though I was only dressed in a singlet and shorts, I sought out my mother and we sheltered at the back of the building all that first night and for the next day or two. Even in Manila it can be chilly on a February night out in the open air. We were lucky enough on that first night to get into a spare room on the ground floor. Along with a host of others, we huddled together for warmth. Moira could not be found and we hoped she was in a place of safety during this dangerous time.

After some hours a young boy, the brother of one of Moira's friends, came quietly up to me and whispered into my ear so that my mother couldn't hear, 'Your sister's been hit.' I immediately thought, my God, blood and carnage, I hope she's not dead. The boy went on to say she was near the main entrance of the building with her friends, talking to the soldiers, when, by the force of an explosion, Moira had been blown into the arms of a GI. She was being treated at the clinic. Her specific instructions were that my mother shouldn't be told immediately as she would be frantic with worry. Shortly after this a very badly shaken, quiet and subdued Moira arrived to join us. A piece of shrapnel had entered her leg but it had been safely removed and all was well.

On that night there was one fatal casualty among our number. A young American lad, Frank H Ward, aged twenty-one-years, was killed. On the following day, the 10 February, as the shelling continued a further four of our ex-internees lost their lives. They were all Americans ranging in age from forty-eight to seventy-years-old. To our relief, on the 11 February we were told it was safe for us to come out of hiding. Intramuros was now in American hands.

With every day that passed, Manila was becoming more secure against enemy attack. By the 18 February it became safe enough to allow ex-internees to go out of the camp for a short distance. Moira and one of her closest friends, Lee Iserson, started to work down at the front gate on that day, granting passes for use within a radius of 300 metres of the camp. To assist them in their work, they were given a list of names of dubious characters who should not be allowed to leave the camp. If any of those individuals applied for a pass, the application should be refused. They performed this task from 2 p.m. to 4 p.m. every afternoon. Moira and her friends had a wonderful time when not on duty. To use her own words, 'We rode around in jeeps, trucks and weapon carriers and flirted with the army. We danced every night until 2 a.m.'

In general, within the camp, life continued in as orderly a fashion as was possible. Ma resumed her work in Santa Catalina hospital, helping to prepare food for the patients. Moira continued to work in the central kitchen in the main building, ladling out the food as before. The great difference was, of course, that the food was appetising and nutritious and everybody was in holiday mood.

Fr Timmons resumed his dinner engagement with me and we sat, as before, in the corridor outside my mother's room on the third floor, next to Mrs Zennor, who never spared us a glance but sat in quiet composure enjoying her food under the new regime. The US army caterers were careful to give us modest portions as we had not been used to eating much for three years and our stomachs wouldn't have been able to cope with large helpings. Seconds would occasionally be given at our evening meal. If we hadn't heard the news but we saw Mrs Zennor get up and scuttle off in great haste with her plate, without mentioning a word to us, we knew that there was more food on offer and would go down to get our second helpings. Because of her secretive behaviour, the devil in me tried to race Mrs Zennor to get in the queue in front of her. There was still an exaggerated fear that the food might run out and so if an extra portion was going you should do your best to get it.

While we remained in camp we were in the safest place in Manila with a strong US military presence protecting us. Outside the camp, the battle for Manila was raging with great ferocity. The retreating Japanese forces were determined to wreak vengeance on the

Filipino people, who had refused to cooperate with them during the occupation. These poor people who had endured three years of looting, hunger, rape and murder during the Japanese occupation were now being butchered by Yamashita's troops for their faithfulness to the Americans during those dreadful years of Japanese rule. This carnage manifested itself with the greatest ferocity south of the river. As the US troops engaged the enemy in North Manila with such speed, there was little the Japanese could do but to demolish everything in their path as they retreated.

In the south of the city it was different. The Japanese had more time while the Americans were mopping up the north of the city, flushing out all enemy resistance there. South of the Pasig River, which flows through the centre of Manila, terrorism reached its height. Crazed groups of Japanese soldiers ran amok, blowing up every installation, building or domestic house, killing men, women and children with great brutality. This bloodbath rivalled the Rape of Nanking. People of both sexes and all ages had their hands tied behind their backs and were bayoneted mercilessly. Their bodies were riddled with bayonet wounds. Others were gunned down while running for safety. Filipino homes and businesses were destroyed. Men, women and children were herded into buildings or warehouses which were blown-up or set on fire. Any who tried to escape were slaughtered. When the US forces occupied the Walled City after overpowering the Japanese, they encountered a most horrific sight. A large number of people had been herded into Fort Santiago just outside the walls and had been sealed up alive within a stone vault. Seven hundred bodies were found. Many Irish priests who had been working in their parishes were forced to hide for days to avoid being killed. Father Kelly was not so lucky. He became a victim of this frenzied killing. One version of events described how the Japanese broke into his church, pinned him to the door with bayonets and then shot him dead. A more authoritative explanation of what happened was described by a Columban priest in The Columban Fathers' publication *Columban Martyrs of Malate*. The priest explained that on 10 February, while the liberation of Manila by American forces was in progress, Fr Kelly and three of his parish fathers plus a few parishioners who were in the Malate church were marched off to the Syquia Apartments, a large building near the church and were not seen again. They were probably moved at night elsewhere and murdered. Their bodies were never found and lie somewhere under the soil of Manila in a nameless grave. The Japanese had set out to make the city one tremendous funeral pyre to bring down the inhabitants of the city with themselves, in their final death throes.

On 23 February, the internees of Los Banos camp were dramatically rescued twenty-five miles behind enemy lines by a most daring raid. There were 6,000 Japanese troops in the Province of Laguna and the largest concentration of those enemy forces was only ten miles from the camp. The prisoners were plucked

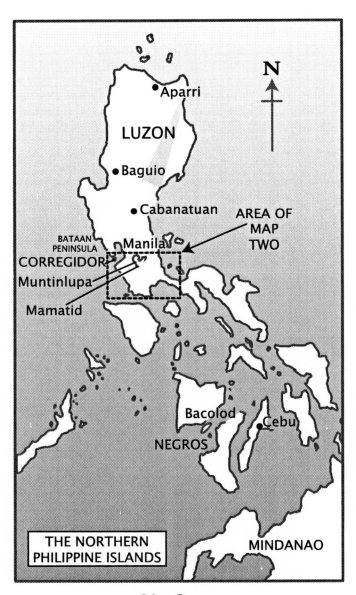

N

Aparri

LUZON

Baguio

Cabanatuan

Manila

AREA OF
MAP
TWO

BATAAN
PENINSULA

CORREGIDOR

Muntinlupa

Mamatid

Bacolod

Cebu

NEGROS

MINDANAO

THE NORTHERN
PHILIPPINE ISLANDS

Map One

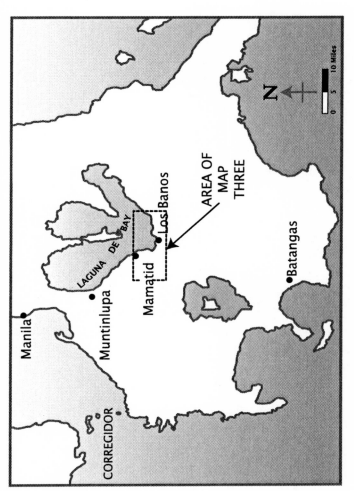

Map Two

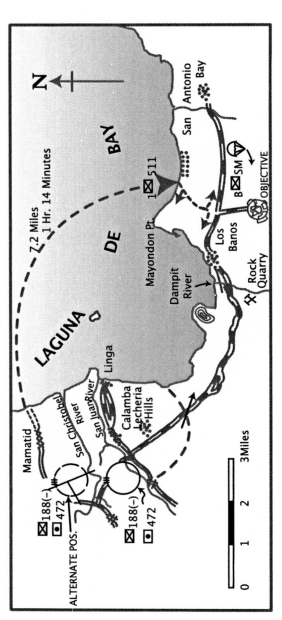

Map Three

from the jaws of death by the simultaneous landing of troops by parachute and from amphibious craft coordinated with an assault by land forces.

The attack on Los Banos started at 7 a.m. This time was chosen as the Japanese guards would be at their morning callisthenics and few would be armed. The drop by the 11th Airborne Division into a pre-arranged field 800 yards from the camp began just before 7 a.m. A division reconnaissance platoon with the help of three escaped internees and a Filipino guerrilla group had smoothed the way for the airborne troops. Part of the reconnaissance group themselves were concealed only fifteen yards from the main gate of the camp. As the airborne drop began, this group, with the help of the Filipinos, fired on the enemy and, a quarter of an hour later, the entire garrison of over 240 Japanese soldiers had been killed.

At the same time, some fifty amphibious tractors had landed on the southern shores of Laguna de Bay, disgorging troops ready to clear the way between the shores of the Laguna and the camp, some three and a half miles away, from which the internees would be carried to safety. They met stiff opposition from the enemy, but the final wave of amphibians who had landed had their way cleared and were able to drive straight to the camp and join up with the parachute infantry and the guerrillas. The US 15th Air Force with their P38 fighter planes provided air cover for the whole rescue operation. Also at 7 a.m. as a back-up should the amphibious arm fail to get to the camp, infantry forces crossed the San Juan river about five miles north-west of Los Banos. They first established a commanding position on the Lecheria Hills and were then able to advance to within two miles of Los Banos. This force was ready to help with the evacuation of internees if required. Happily, their services were not needed. By 7.20 a.m. the paratroopers had reached the camp. After an excited first few moments, the internees were told to pack in five minutes and be ready to get out. They were to take only what they could carry.

In the meantime, the Filipinos had put a torch to the Japanese quarters and the guardhouses and the flames were quickly spreading to the rest of the camp. Amphibious trucks were waiting at the gate to take the inhabitants of the camp to the lake and across the water to safety. Most of the internees were accommodated by this transport, but about fifty were required to make their way on foot to the lakeside dragging their luggage along the best way they could. This party of weak and shaky individuals were looked after well and helped on their dangerous journey to the shore.

The passage to Mamatid in American held territory was about seven miles north across the lake. It took two hours to get there. Safe at last, 2,146 US citizens, British and other allied personnel had been rescued in a most spectacular operation. A further eighteen miles by trucks heading north up the coast brought the ex-internees to Muntinlupa where they could recuperate and, if necessary, receive hospital care.

Moira received a first-hand blow-by-blow account of

the rescue from Jim Innes, one of her friends who had moved to Los Banos from Santo Tomas in early 1944. Jim was among those who had to haul their luggage to the lake. He was worn out when he reached the beach – he only had bananas and coconuts to eat. As they waited by the shore for transport across the water by the returning amphibians, they were told to jettison their luggage and take only what they could wear or stuff into their pockets. Like the others, Jim finally arrived at Muntinlupa exhausted but happy. To add to his pleasure he received his discarded luggage, as did all the others, in very short order after their arrival.

Throughout the whole exercise, casualties were very light for the rescuers: two killed and three wounded. In addition, three internees were slightly hurt. Given the meticulous planning and complete secrecy observed throughout, the key to the successful execution of the rescue was the utter surprise and speed with which it was carried out. The mission was regarded as one of the most perfectly timed and coordinated of the Philippines campaign.

At this point, it may be of interest to note that the story of Santo Tomas internment camp and that of Los Banos, contained in a book published in 1975 entitled *Prisoners of Santo Thomas*, by Celia Lucas, was used as background material for the popular TV series 'Tenko'.

Back in Manila, at the beginning of March 1945 the US forces declared the city to be secure. Movement within Manila could at last take place in safety and the big process of reconstruction could begin.

The President of the Philippines, Manuel Quezon, had died in the USA during the occupation of his country by Japan. His successor, President Sergio Osmena, who had been living in Washington DC, was invited to wade ashore with General MacArthur's party at the initial landing in the Philippines on the island of Leyte in December 1944. With the capture of Manila by the US army, the Philippine President returned again from Washington and took over the reins of civil government from the military administration of General MacArthur in a ceremony at Malacanan Palace.

A New Life

Arrangements were now going apace to repatriate the ex-internees of our camp. Most of them were Americans and they were the first to leave. In due course it was the turn of the British. Early in the morning of 8 April 1945, the main body of the British ex-prisoners and a residue of Americans who didn't get on the earlier repatriation ships emerged from all parts of the camp to assemble in front of the main building, clutching their few possessions. US army trucks were waiting to take us to Manila harbour for the start of our journey home.

As I stood there with my mother and Moira, I had mixed feelings. I was excited at the thought of a new life in England but was apprehensive about this very different world I would have to fit in to and what my relations, whom I had never seen, would be like. Thinking about our immediate journey to the ship, I tried to put myself in the shoes of those in our group who had lived in Manila before the Japanese occupation. I was sure that the prospect of travelling through the city, which had been their home and was now in ruins, promised to be a heart-rending experience. For us, however, who hadn't known Manila before the war, it was different. All we wanted to do was to leave the death and destruction behind, get on our ship and head for the States on the first leg of our journey to England.

In Manila Bay, the US troopship *Admiral E W Eberle*, was waiting to take us across the Pacific Ocean to Los Angeles, California. The journey to America was expected to take a little more than three weeks. The war was still in progress in Europe, victory for the Allies would occur in a month. Against Japan, the war would continue until the middle of August ending abruptly with the dropping of the atomic bombs on the Japanese cities of Hiroshima and Nagasaki. Our sea voyage across the Pacific in April promised to be perfectly safe as the Japanese naval power had been broken and the remnants of their navy had gone north to protect their homeland in the dying months of the war.

After finding my sleeping quarters on the ship, I went on deck to meet my mother and Moira. It was wonderful to get out in the fresh air. All the other passengers must have felt the same way. The decks were packed with people. We set sail on the 10 April and were escorted across the Pacific to Honolulu by two destroyers. To entertain us on our journey, we had Rudy Valet's band and to our delight they played for us every afternoon. I enjoyed being on deck but found when going down below the atmosphere was very oppressive. It is true in April the weather was getting warm, but I was used to that, so why did I feel so wretched below deck? I put it down to the movement of the ship and the smell of paint, which seems to be ever-present on ships. A few days before starting our voyage I had cut my foot playing basketball barefooted in the camp. This cut made no impact on me at the time, nor did I later connect it with my feeling unwell on board ship. The cut seems to have remained dormant for two to three weeks. However, about a fortnight out from Manila, I had started running a temperature and on examining my left leg, which was hurting now, I saw a long red streak running up from my ankle. I had a pain in my groin on the left side, as my body was fighting a battle to the death against the poison advancing up my leg. On going to the clinic for treatment, the doctor on duty, seeing the state I was in, admitted me immediately to the ship's hospital. How lucky I was – I was treated with penicillin, the new antibiotic – the wonder drug. It immediately attacked my poisoned leg and within a few days my fever had gone and the poison had been sucked out of my body. I was well again.

Looking out of the porthole on the morning I was due to leave the hospital, I was so excited to see land in the distance. This was America. We were heading for Los Angeles and in a very short time we docked at San Pedro. As we sailed into port our band struck up 'California, Here I Come' and a band on the quayside took up the same theme. There was great excitement and the whole occasion was charged with emotion. I was quickly discharged from the hospital and joined Ma and Moira on deck with my luggage. We had a long wait ahead of us. We didn't disembark until late in the afternoon. We were taken to the municipal hall. There were an exhaustive army of forms to be completed, followed by fingerprinting of every passenger from the babe in arms to the octogenarian. This was bureaucracy at its worst. Finally, at about 2 a.m. we were driven into Los Angeles and given accommodation at the Hotel Hayward. Fr McMullen took me under his wing. I shared a room with him for the remainder of the night. I didn't sleep a wink. By 8 a.m. the next morning we British boarded a train, especially provided for us, to journey eastbound for Halifax, Nova Scotia. It was a most fascinating trip travelling through the varied American countryside.

On Sunday 6 May, as our railroad took us through the outskirts of the towns, it seemed to me that the occupants of the houses bordering the tracks were all out in their gardens with the deliberate intention of watching us chug by. Perhaps they knew we were ex-prisoners of the Japanese being repatriated. In any event they waved enthusiastically as we passed by and we responded with equal enthusiasm at their friendliness. It was, after all, a very exciting time for everyone. The war in Europe was all but over and people were getting in holiday mood. On Tuesday we crossed the border into Canada at London, Ontario. Union flags were fluttering everywhere. Throngs of people on either side of our train in great excitement were waving their flags and shouting, 'The war's over, the war's over'. V E day had come at last and we all thanked God that at least in Europe it was all over. On the 10 May we arrived in Halifax, Nova Scotia, and were immediately taken aboard the Cunard ship, SS *Scythia*, waiting to take us to England. After a relaxing journey across the Atlantic we arrived at Liverpool on the afternoon of Friday 25 May. We were to disembark the next morning for the last few miles of our journey to London. To while away the time after dinner, we played deck quoits late into the evening. Looking across the bay to the Liver Building clock, I was amazed to see it was 11 p.m. and it was still light. This was our first experience of Double summer time. The next morning we negotiated customs with the minimum of formality and boarded the train for Euston. As we got close to London Ma, who was normally very composed, started to get excited. She was returning home to see her family again after so many years abroad. The train arrived at Euston station mid afternoon. Moira was quick to spot Maudie and Beryl, my mother's sisters, on the platform. In no time we had joined them. After a happy reunion we all set off for Muswell Hill in North London to stay with Maudie and Granny in their two-bedroomed flat until we were able to find a place of our own to live. Ma was home after nearly twenty years in the Far East. Moira and I would have to adjust to a new way of life. The future held many unanswered questions. As time unfolded, these questions might resolve themselves. For the time being we had a roof over our heads, living happily with Ma's family.

Internees in China

While we had been experiencing camp life under the Japanese in the Philippines, Pop and the rest of the Malone family were learning how to cope with enemy occupation in China.

On the 8 December 1941, following their attack on Pearl Harbor, the Japanese seized control of the International Settlement and the French Concession in Shanghai. Taking a leaf out of Nazi Germany's book relating to the Jews, Western enemy residents throughout China were ordered to wear red armbands at all times. The British had a large 'B' on their bands, plus a personal number. Most of the British community in Peking moved into the British Legation. Their lives went on in an acceptable way, as a temporary arrangement, provided they always remembered to wear their armbands when they went out into the city. In other parts of China, foreign residents gathered together and pooled their food and other essentials so as to live as economically as possible. In Shanghai early in 1942, the Japanese rounded up and imprisoned leaders of the business community in an interrogation centre in Haiphong Road. As for the Jewish refugees, already in their ghetto in Shanghai, they suffered also with the entry of Japan into the Second World War. Their rations were cut, the school was closed down and their houses ransacked in an attempt to find short wave radios.

On the 25 March 1943 in Peking, the residents of the British Legation were ordered to a camp 200 miles away in Weihsien in Shantung province. It was a camp for British and American 'enemy' residents of North China. When the Peking contingent arrived at the camp they found the European inhabitants of Tientsin and Tsingtao and other North China cities and towns already there. At about the same time, the foreign enemy residents scattered throughout South China, including Canton where Pop was still living, were transferred to Shanghai. These foreigners, together with the Shanghai enemy civilians, were being assembled before being despatched to the numerous camps in and around the city. Pop soon joined his sisters, Aggie and Maudie, and was in time to accompany them to Yangchow camp in the spring of 1943. He told them that just before he left Canton he was able to find a good home for Bob, our English setter. A kind German gentleman was willing to take him. Rangi, the 'outside dog' was left to work out his own salvation, poor creature. Likewise, the aunties were able to find a suitable person to look after their two Pekinese dogs, Puck and Baby. The budgerigar Bobo was taken to the local pet shop.

All the civilian prisoners were told to prepare a bed and bedroll, to be transferred later to their camp, and three suitcases to include food and clothing for four days. Those for Yangchow camp were ordered to assemble at Holy Trinity Cathedral to be labelled and sorted. George and his wife Nina were destined for another camp in the Shanghai area and did not go to the cathedral assembly point. The Yangchow group were then taken through the muddy waters of the Wangpoo River out into the Yellow Sea to the China Inland Mission Hospital in Yangchow. The dormitories at Yangchow were so arranged that families shared the smaller rooms on the ground floor and rooms for unattached men or women were situated on the floor above. The space allocated for each person was sufficient only for a bed and mosquito net. The bed and bedding, which was to follow the arrival of the internees, didn't appear for several days, which meant that those in the camp would have to sleep on bare boards in the meantime. Washing was a problem. There was no running water and each individual was rationed to a bucket of cold canal water a day. This was to be used for washing clothes as well as for personal use. As time went on, the water ration was considerably reduced. There was no heating and in the depths of winter it brought great hardship for everyone. In fact, in the winter of 1944/5 the temperature dropped to 14°F and Pop suffered from frozen feet. This frostbite forced him to take to his bed for six weeks before he recovered. The food was rationed to 900 calories a day. This took the form of watery rice in the morning, containing an ample supply of cooked weevils, not unlike our mush in Santo Tomas. In the evening watery stew was supplied, with a few strands of vegetables and some scraps of pork if you were lucky. A sought after occupation in the camp was kitchen duty as it gave the opportunity of spiriting away a carrot or some other vegetable for later. These conditions were endured by Pop and his two sisters, Aunties Aggie and Maudie, until the end of the war in August 1945.

The war had been brought to an abrupt end by the dropping of the atomic bombs, but the end of hostilities brought a mixed blessing for the foreigners living in China. Most of them, who had been interned, could see nothing much left for them in China and sought repatriation. They could not return to their old style of living, which had been swept away on 11 January 1943 when the British ambassador in Chungking signed the Sino–British Treaty which returned the remaining concessions and foreign settlements to China. At the same time, a similar treaty was signed between America and China in Washington.

The Soviet Union which always had its eye to the main chance, had declared war on Japan on 8 August 1945, a few days before the Japanese surrender to the Allies. This action emboldened the Chinese Communists, with the backing of their Soviet masters, to flout the orders of the Military Council of the Chinese Government. All armed forces in the country were to remain where they were and to await orders relating to the surrender. The Chinese Communists, taking advantage of the lull, moved their soldiers into strategic positions and seized control of the main railway systems of China, ostensibly to accept the surrender of local Japanese forces. In fact, their objective was to place themselves in advantageous positions in anticipation of the civil war which they would provoke against Generalissimo Chiang Kai-shek's Nationalist government. They intended to revive the conflicts they had had with the Nationalist forces reaching back to the 1920s. Their purpose was, as before, to defeat Chiang and set up a Communist regime. This situation did not bode well for the old China hands who, like the Malone family, wanted to continue living in that country as long as it was possible to do so.

The civil war did materialise and was fought with great vigour on both sides. The Communists got the upper hand and, by 1949, had driven Chiang and his Nationalist armies out of mainland China and set up a Communist regime. The Nationalists accepted defeat and retired to the island of Taiwan (Formosa).

On release from the camp in Yangchow, Pop and Aunties Aggie and Maudie were unable to return to their pre-war homes and were accommodated at Farren's, 325 Great Western Road, Shanghai, along with those waiting for repatriation. Towards the end of January 1946, the aunties, and for a short time Pop, were transferred to Ash Camp, further down the same road. This camp, many years before, was used by British troops. It was a collection of huts with very small grubby little rooms. There was no furniture provided except what had been left behind by the army. The aunties found in their room two army cots, two metal chairs, one half canvas half wooden chair and a small rough wooden table. To provide a sideboard and dressing table they stood their trunks on end. The only saving grace in all this was that the food was good.

Within days of their arrival at Ash Camp, Farren's closed down as most of the residents there left on the repatriation ship *The Highland Chieftain* on the 1 February. There were 1,200 on board, former internees both from Shanghai and Tientsin. Those who remained were transferred to Ash Camp.

Before the end of 1945, Pop was promised employment with Jardine Matheson's as a purser on the SS *Kutwo* as soon as she had been released by the Chinese authorities. The ship, when overhauled and refurbished, would travel up and down the Yangtze River between Shanghai and Hankow.

Uncle George and his wife Nina, who had been pushed from pillar to post in one centre after another, joined the others in Ash Camp for a short while. George had worked for the Shanghai municipal council. After the war as the council had been handed over to the Chinese, all foreigners formerly employed there lost their jobs. George tried to get some other employment but as jobs for foreigners were scarce he decided to opt for repatriation. Repatriates were told they would be assisted to find employment in England on their arrival. There appeared to be no alternative for him. He sailed for England with Nina on the P&O ship, the SS *Strathmore* on the 29 March 1946.

Pop started his work with Jardine's early in March 1946. He lived on the SS *Kutwo* while in dock in Shanghai for its overhaul but went ashore each day to the office to help out in the passenger department. This venture didn't last very long. The preparation of the *Kutwo* for its scheduled passage between Shanghai and Hankow, so far as Pop was concerned, came to nothing. In April he was suddenly despatched down south to Swatow for another shore job.

In the meantime, the aunties managed the best way they could in Ash Camp. But life was hard in post-war China. As time went on, the cost of living rose steeply and seemed to be spiralling out of control. They avoided shopping as much as possible as the prices in the shops were prohibitive. Also they were forced to continue living in the camp as any accommodation in Shanghai or elsewhere was far beyond their means. On top of this, the civil war between the Communists and the Nationalists, which had begun shortly after the end of the Second World War, was in full spate by the middle of 1946 and threatened to engulf the whole country. Auntie Maudie in a letter to Moira in August 1946 said how she and Auntie Aggie loved China and nothing short of an earthquake would have made them leave it for good. However, with heavy hearts they had decided to take such a step as living conditions in China had become impossible for them. By August my father had been given a new job for Jardine's in Tientsin, one of the important cities of North China. He was approaching his mid sixties and would have to think of retiring in the not-too-distant future. He would have loved my mother, Moira and me to come back to China so that we could live there again as a family after our long separation. However, like his sisters, he too was reluctantly coming to the conclusion that the future for foreigners in China looked very bleak indeed and there seemed no other course but to leave the country.

Once the aunties had made the decision to be repatriated they began to gather together all their furniture and other domestic items which they had stored for the duration of the war. There would be only a limited amount of luggage they could take with them. Large items, such as their blackwood furniture, together with a few trunks with household effects would have to go separately. The APC would pay the freight for those larger items. The aunties expected to sail for England on the *Empress of Australia* at the end of October and arrive at their destination in the first half of December. They had no idea where they would be sent to live on their arrival in England. In the event, they did get a passage on the *Empress of Australia* and, to their delight, Pop was able to join them. They left Shanghai at the end of October and docked at Liverpool early in December. George and Nina, who had left for England earlier in 1946 had been taken to Blakeshall Hostel in Kidderminster, Worcestershire. Pop and our aunts were taken there as well. This accommodation, set in the beautiful English countryside, was to be their temporary home until they found somewhere of their own to live.

George was still at Blakeshall and when his brother and sisters arrived, he and Nina had a great reunion with them. Pop had reached England in poor health with little savings and no job. The aunties seemed to be in a fitter condition and their financial situation was sounder in that Auntie Maudie had some savings and a regular pension from the APC. All of them had to face a challenging new life in England. The most important thing on Pop's list of priorities was to get a place to live, probably in London where we could be all together as a family. From the time we left Canton at the beginning of December 1941 until the end of the war in 1945, Ma had received no communication from him or from any other member of the Malone family in China. Pop had, however, received one short letter from Ma at the beginning of 1942 telling him that we were interned in a camp in Manila in the Philippines.

The Malone family's arrival in England after over fifty years in China, closed one very long chapter in their lives and opened a new one. The resilience they had shown in coping with difficult situations in the Far East would surely not desert them now in the calmer waters of life in this country.

Sixty Years On

A lot of water has flowed under the bridge since the events I have been describing in these pages. I will attempt to explain briefly how the Malone family managed to settle in this country after so many years abroad and what became of them in the years that followed.

Ma, Moira and I arrived from Euston Station with Maudie and Beryl to an emotional but happy occasion as we crossed the threshold of Granny and Maudie's flat in Muswell Hill.

It was wonderful for Ma to be able to live with her mother until we could find somewhere else for ourselves. However, in the meantime, we would be crowding them out. Ma shared Granny's double bed and a camp bed was found for me, to be used in the dining room. Moira was very fortunate to be offered a room by good friends of the family, Mr and Mrs Tudball, in their house across the road.

By this time I was fifteen and a half years old and had missed a great deal of schooling. I resumed my studies by attending the Jesuit school, St Ignatius College, Stamford Hill, N15, starting in September 1945. I was placed in a class with boys two years younger than I was. However, my sporting activities in camp stood me in good stead and compensated for my

The author in England, 1946

lack of academic work. I took to rugby with great relish at school and with some success. Our first fifteen was a strong side and did well against good opposition. This led me into playing club rugby with the London Irish and the Bank of England for a number of years, which I thoroughly enjoyed. Moira, who was seventeen years old in June, was sent to St George's secretarial college in Russell Square. On the job front, Ma was particularly fortunate. She applied to the Alliance Assurance Company in Wigmore Street, London, where she had worked before going to China and was accepted immediately. She returned to the same job she had held twenty years before as bookkeeper for the branch. She resumed her old seat and picked up the same pen, so to speak, that she had put down so many years before and started again, as though she had just been out for lunch!

Moira had obtained a secretarial post after her training and did very well in this pursuit. Among other positions, she became a senior secretary at the British Sugar Corporation. Later she worked for International Business Machines UK (IBM, UK) as secretary to the head of the Customer Engineers Department. In my case, I left school in 1950 and joined the Bank of England. It was undoubtedly the best thing I did in my life. It was quite fortuitous how it came about. I had no clear idea of what I wanted to do and applied for a number of jobs. While I was doing this, a friend of the family, Freda Leeds, visited Granny's flat. She was employed at the Bank of England and asked what I was going to do now that I had left school. She said, if I hadn't settled on anything, perhaps I should apply to the Bank of England – they were recruiting at that time. I applied and was accepted. If I had not taken her advice, I should not have met Margaret Heffernan, a lovely girl with an engaging smile. We were married in June 1957 at St Dunstan's Church, Gunnersbury Avenue, Acton.

The aunties, Maudie and Aggie, within a year of their arrival in Blakeshall Hostel in Kidderminster, were able to buy a two-bedroomed bungalow at Carpenders Park, near Watford. As we in Muswell Hill had not yet been able to find any accommodation to rent which was within our means, Pop joined his sisters in their new home. By this time, George and his wife Nina had moved from Blakeshall to Coventry where he had managed to obtain a job.

We stayed with Granny and Maudie until 1954, when we were able at last to rent a flat in Queens Avenue, Muswell Hill. Pop joined us. It was the first time that we had been together as a family since Canton in 1941. This, however, was a short-lived reunion. I left home in 1957 when I married Margaret. I am glad that Pop was able to attend the wedding, although he hadn't been well since returning from the Far East. Among our wedding guests was Jim Clifford, a customer engineer in IBM. He was Margaret's first cousin. Moira knew him slightly as she was working in the same department in IBM. Their friendship blossomed and in 1962 they were married.

Margaret and I bought our first house in Hounslow. It was while we were living there that Michael Desmond was born in West Middlesex Hospital, Isleworth in January 1959. He was followed by Patricia Mary in August 1960. We moved to Ealing in 1961 and Anthony John was born there in November 1962. In August 1966 Helen Margaret arrived to complete our family.

Moira and Jim had four children also. First, Dominic, then Tim, Bernadette followed and lastly Matthew.

In March 1958, Pop died in Queens Avenue. He had never really settled in England and the rigours of internment must have taken their toll. He was seventy-five years of age.

The Aunties, Aggie and Maudie would have preferred to end their days in China. However, they lived quietly in their bungalow in Carpenders Park with Pop as company during their first few years there. They both died in the early 1960s. Auntie Aggie was a semi invalid in the last few years of her life and spent most of the day in bed. Auntie Maudie ran the bungalow. They had a little dog which Maudie took out for its walk each day and so she was regularly seen by her neighbours. Suddenly she didn't appear for several days and her next door neighbour became concerned and tried, but failed, to discover what might have happened. She called the police. They broke into the bungalow to find the two ladies dead in the bedroom. Aggie was in bed, Maudie was lying face downwards on the ground with her head towards the bed. Possibly Maudie came into the bedroom, saw what had happened to Aggie and the shock killed her. Ma was quite shaken when she heard what had happened. She and I went to identify the bodies and to arrange the funeral. They were buried in a cemetery in Carpenders Park. A sad end for the two aunties.

George and Nina lived in Coventry. We didn't see a great deal of them. George worked for a car firm. He once told us that he used to bet on the horses and was singularly successful. In fact, he earned more from this pastime than he was paid in his job. All his workmates were amazed at his skill and were constantly asking him for tips. Poor George was standing at a bus stop in the late 1950s when he collapsed. He died almost instantly. His wife Nina had suffered from goitre for many years. In February 1957 she was accepted as a patient in the Central Mental Hospital near Warwick and died there of bronchopneumonia in September 1959.

Over the years after internment, Moira, a good letter writer, kept in touch with a number of her friends living in the States. Lee Clee (née Iserson) was a particular friend whom she corresponded with for years. I was quite different. Letter writing was not my forte. I left the old life behind and struggled to keep abreast of the new.

Shortly after Moira left Queens Avenue to get married, a flat in Eveline Court became available. This was in the block of flats where we had lived with Granny and Maudie for so many years. Ma took it right away and was pleased to be living in Eveline Court again and close to her mother and Maudie. After living there for a few years, Moira asked Ma to come and live with them. They had bought a large house in Chorleywood and there would be plenty of room. While living in Chorleywood, Jim was seconded to Paris for a three-year stint. The family plus Ma left for Saint-Cloud to the west of Paris in 1975. The French house accom-modated them all very comfortably. The children went to the English school in Paris.

Our family was invited to Paris each Christmas while the Cliffords were there. We visited the sights, saw some of the nightlife of Paris, travelled to Versailles which was only a few miles by train from St Cloud and generally enjoyed the hospitality we were offered. At the end of the three years, all four of Moira and Jim's children had become fluent in French – to my knowledge they have retained that fluency to this day. Shortly before Jim had completed his three years in Paris Ma became ill. She didn't live long enough to be able to return to England and died in Saint Cloud on the 19 March 1978, aged eighty-one years.

The Cliffords came back to this country later on in 1978. They had developed quite an attraction for France during their stay. A few years later, in 1985 Moira and Jim were on holiday in Paris. One Sunday morning while walking to Mass, being a bit late, they hurried to get there in time. This vigorous exercise seemed to have been too much for Moira. During the service, she collapsed. An ambulance took her to hospital. She was dead on arrival. This was a terrible shock for the whole family. Moira was fifty-seven-years-old at her death. Jim phoned home to England to give the sad news to his family. I went over to Chorleywood to help in any way I could. Jim could not return immediately as he was required to arrange for Moira's body to be brought home. Matthew, the youngest of the family, to his credit, took over the arrangements for the funeral. I was impressed with his determination to do the best for his mother, which included finding a very attractive cemetery for her at Amersham.

Having moved to Ealing in the early sixties, we have lived there ever since. Our children have grown up there. Michael is a research chemist living in Macclesfield, Cheshire, working for Astra Zeneca. Patricia did secretarial work in NatWest Bank for a number of years. She married Christopher O'Rourke, an employee of Fiat, the Italian car firm. They have two children, James and Victoria. Anthony, after his degree in accounting and statistics is now a computer consultant. While working in the merchant bank Schroders, he met Nicky Salvatori. They married in 1996 and have three children: Jessica, Gabriel and Francesca. Helen, a Physics graduate, turned her attention to the information industry. She is now an information manager at GlaxoSmithKline and lives with her fiancé Dermot McBride in Ashford, Middlesex.

From the foregoing account you can see that I am the last to survive of the Malone family who lived in the Far East. Did I learn anything in those turbulent wartime days that I might not have done otherwise? During my time in the internment camp, what I had missed in formal education, I had acquired in the university of life. One thing I became aware of was that when the veneer of civilised living is removed, in extreme circumstances, the best and worst in people are revealed. This facet of human nature showed itself to me very clearly in those trying days. In many ways I am glad to have had the opportunity of learning about life in a prison camp and how people reacted to their circumstances. However, I would not wish to repeat the experience, for all the tea in China!

Bibliography

Books

Duus, Peter [ed.], *The Cambridge History of Japan: vol. 6, The Twentieth Century*, Cambridge University Press, 1988

Fairbank and Twitchett [ed.], *The Cambridge History of China: vol. 10, Late Ching: 1800–1911*, Cambridge University Press, 1978

Fairbank, John K [ed.], *The Cambridge History of China: vol. 12, Republican China: 1912–1949*, Cambridge University Press, 1983

Hibbert, Christopher, *The Dragon Wakes: China and the West 1793–1911*, Essex, Longmans, 1970

Chiang Kai-shek, *Soviet Russia in China: A Summing-up at Seventy*, New York, Farrar, Straus and Cudahy, 1958

Lucas, Celia, *Prisoners of Santo Tomas: Civilian Prisoners of the Japanese*, Barnsley, Pen and Sword Books, 1999

McCall, James E, *Santo Tomas Internment Camp: Stic in Verse and Reverse Stic-toons and Stic-tislics*, Lincoln, Nebraska, Woodruff Printing Co., 1945

O'Brien, Fr Niall [ed.], *Columban Martyrs of Malate*, Kadena Press Inc., 1995

Prising, Robin, *Manila, Goodbye*, London, Heinemann, 1976

Wood, Frances, *No Dogs and not many Chinese: Treaty Port Life in China 1843–1943*, London, John Murray, 2000

Wright-Nooth, George; Adkin, Mark, *Prisoner of the*

Turnip Heads: The Fall of Hong Kong and Imprisonment by the Japanese, London, Cassell, 2002

Other

Free Philippines, newspaper launched 9 February 1945 with copies up to 7 April 1945, as General MacArthur Frees Manila

Sundry family letters

Printed in the United Kingdom
by Lightning Source UK Ltd.
115439UKS00001B/82-99